Linguistic Approaches to the Romance Lexicon

Frank H. Nuessel, Jr.

Editor

Georgetown University Press, Washington, D.C. 20057

Library of Congress Cataloging in Publication Data

Approaches to the Lexicon Conference, University of
   Louisville, 1978.
   Linguistic approaches to the Romance lexicon.

   "Held at the University of Louisville ... under
the sponsorship of the College of Arts and Sciences,
the Interdisciplinary Linguistics Program, and the
Department of Modern Languages."
   1. Romance languages--Congresses. 2. Romance
languages--Lexicology--Congresses. I. Nuessel,
Frank H. II. Louisville, Ky. University. College
of Arts and Sciences. III. Louisville, Ky.
University. Dept. of Modern Languages.
PC11.A67 1978   440   78-12654
ISBN 0-87840-046-X

Copyright © 1978 by Georgetown University
All rights reserved
Printed in the United States of America

International Standard Book Number: 0-87840-046-X

To my mother,

RITA E. NUESSEL

CONTENTS

PREFACE	v
C. Arthur Brakel Morphophonology in the generative lexicon	1
Charles Elerick The bilingual lexicon and linguistic innovation	12

Lee Ann Grace
   Indigenisms in Mexican Spanish:
     A sociolinguistic approach
	22

Carl Kirschner
   Lexical decomposition of complex verb
     roots in Spanish
	30

John Lihani
   A literary jargon of early Spanish drama:
     The Sayagués dialect
	39

Raleigh Morgan, Jr.
   Lexical correspondences between metropolitan
     and Canadian French
	45

Dorothy A. Rissel Cognitive styles in Spanish and English	60

Mordecai Rubin
   Considerations of the English and home
     subdialect environments for the teaching
     of Spanish to Spanish-dominant bilingual
     children
	68

Gladys E. Saunders
  A linguistic typology of dictionaries:
    With reference to French   77

John J. Staczek
  Degapping the lexicon of Spanish verbs   90

Bruce G. Stiehm
  Cultural values and lexical features
    in Spanish grammar   98

Sonia Ramírez Wohlmuth
  Lexicalization of the irregular past
    participle in Hispano-Romance up to
    and including the Alfonsine period   105

PREFACE

The present volume contains the proceedings of the Approaches to the Lexicon Conference held at the University of Louisville on March 10-11, 1978, under the sponsorship of the College of Arts and Sciences, the Interdisciplinary Linguistics Program, and the Department of Modern Languages. The papers relate to specific analyses of three Romance languages: nine deal with Spanish, two with French, and one with Portuguese. Each study seeks to provide novel insights into the various problems and issues of the Romance lexicon. Clearly, a divergency of methodology characterizes these 12 essays concerning lexicological phonemena. More precisely, the analytical procedures employed by these lingusts include diachronic and synchronic accounts within structural and transformational frameworks as well as sociolinguistic and dialectal descriptions.

I wish to acknowledge the aid and support of John A. Dillon, Jr., Vice President for Academic Affairs; Arthur J. Slavin, Dean of the College of Arts and Sciences; David R. Hershberg, Chairman of the Department of Modern Languages; my colleague, James D. Anderson; and the members of the selection committee --Robert H. Kimball, John Robinson, William Schuyler, Robert N. St. Clair, and R. Margaret Wilhite. In addition, I wish to thank Marcia Adams for her assistance in the organization of the conference.

I hope that the readers of this volume will find the various analytical perspectives to be useful references as well as points of departure for additional research inspired by the sound scholarship of these essays.

Frank H. Nuessel, Jr.

University of Louisville

MORPHOPHONOLOGY IN THE
GENERATIVE LEXICON

C. ARTHUR BRAKEL
State University of New York, Albany

Purpose. The controlling purpose of this paper is to examine two currently fashionable tenets of generative theory: the word as the base for further word formation and the naturalness of underlying representation.
   Generative theoreticians have wavered on the abstract nature of the bases of operations for transformational rules. Early syntactic theory envisioned kernel sentences (surface structures) as the base of all optional transformations; however this approach proved counterproductive inasmuch as obligatory transformations had to apply to produce kernel sentences, then optional transformations applied, after which the same obligatory transformations reapplied in what was, perhaps, a prototype of the transformational cycle. Theoreticians eliminated a step from sentence generation and increased descriptive adequacy when they agreed that abstract base markers would furnish the raw material for obligatory and optional transformations.
   Morphological theory has proceeded in a mirror image of syntactic theory. Theoreticians first envisioned the lexicon as a catalogue of all the morphemes of a language; these morphemes appeared with boundary symbols and were combined to form words or to provide the proper inflected shape for a string of morphemes (i.e. a word) in a specific syntactic environment. Indeed, morphological processes acted on bases which were, at times, so abstract that they contained totally unspecified vowels and consonants or segments which had no direct manifestation in the surface phonology of the language in question. There has been a retreat from this position to one in which lexical representation is motivated by the

surface phonology--polymorphemic as well as monomorphemic words are lexical entries and the bases for word forming processes and for all phonological operations.

Linguists believe morphology to be more abstract than phonology, yet less abstract than syntax. Indeed it is the focal point in the grammar of any language; it is the point at which abstract grammatical structure and human articulatory capabilities converge, where universal patterns of grammar and of sound structure become language-specific. Generativists have been in a quandary concerning the localization of morphology in the standard model, and have decided that the proper place for this least abstract subsystem of grammatical structure which is coupled with the most abstract level of sound structure is the lexicon. It is imperative that a model of the generative lexicon be proposed in line with the constraints in vogue today. These are valid and useful constraints, yet no one has bothered to create a model that articulates the consequences of the dicta current in generative theory. Once a model has been outlined, we can examine the consequences of recent dicta (see Scheme 1).

The most articulate formulation, in English, of the role of morphology in the lexicon of generative grammar is Mark Aronoff's Word Formation in Generative Grammar.[1] The central hypothesis of this work is:

> All regular word-formation processes are word-based. A new word is formed by applying a regular [sic] rule to a single already existing word. Both the new word and the existing one are members of major lexical categories. (Aronoff 1976:21)

He elaborates (p. 22):

> The rules of word formation are rules for generating words which may be stored in the dictionary of a language ... these rules are completely separate from the syntactic and phonological rules ... when a WFR specifies a phonological operation ... [it] is part of the WFR itself.

Later (p. 23), he says: '... each word may be entered in the dictionary as a fully specified separate item ...' and (p. 85) 'A WFR ... operate[s] on a base, ... a word, ... a fully specified phonological entity of unique form'. He concludes (p. 23) that 'This theory ... rid[s] us of the central problem of a morpheme based theory of morphology' which is, according to Aronoff, the definition of a morpheme as a unit of meaning. Such a definition is misleading since many recognizable morphemes have no constant meaning and only acquire meaning in the context of other morphemes, i.e. in words.

Scheme 1. The Generative Model of the Lexicon.[2]

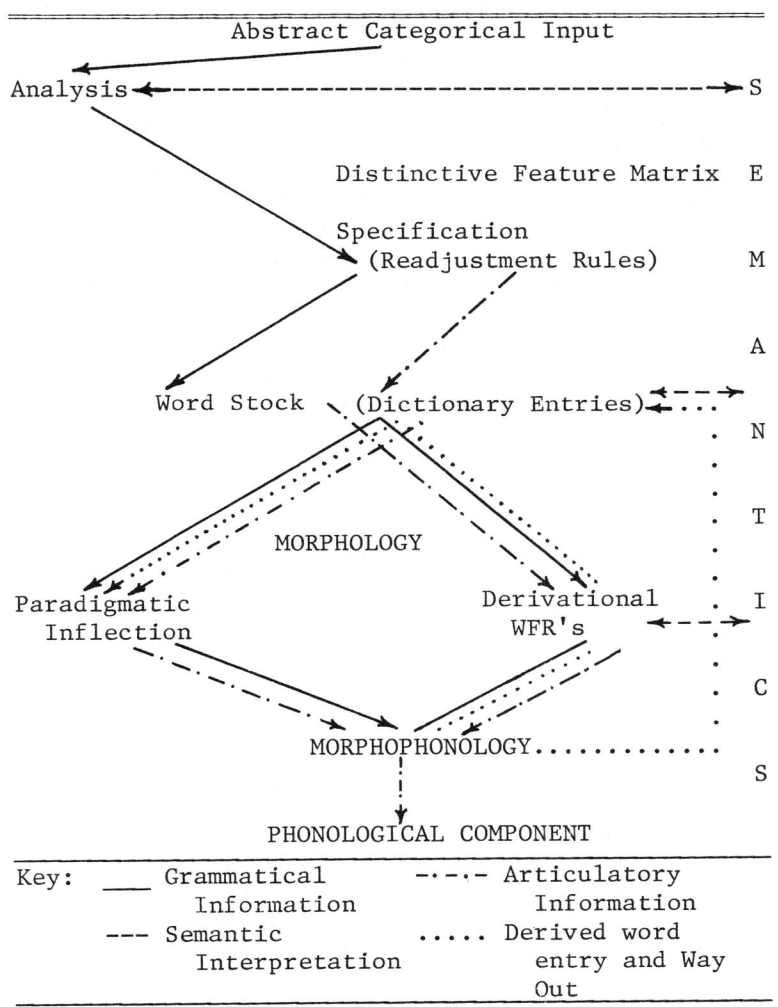

The +sume of resume, consume, and presume cannot be said to have a constant meaning.

Aronoff claims that the rules of morphology, contrary to the rules of syntax and phonology are normally held in abeyance during the production of sentences, that they are '... merely rules for adding to and, derivatively, analyzing ... [dictionary] entries' (Aronoff 1976:46).[3] Of course they may be invoked by the native speaker in the creation of neologisms which will be immediately intelligible if the forms used occur elsewhere and if the rules of word formation are obeyed. Such creation and analysis evoke the ability, held to be remarkable, of native speakers to create and understand original, unique, never before heard, grammatical, utterances. He divides morphophonological rules into adjustment rules, rules which delete parts of stems and bases, and allomorphy rules which modify phonological specifications of stems, bases, and affixes. His concentration is on derivational morphology, where the addition of affixes transforms the form class of preexisting words: e.g. industry$_N$ → industrial$_{Adj}$ → industrialize$_{Vb}$ → industrialization$_N$. His tack assumes that simple (nonderived) words are the base for such operations and that all modifications, adjustments, and allomorphies are the result of word forming processes. Related words such as list (1) have their vowel qualities changed (1,7 äy → I; 2 ey → ä; 3, 10 iy → ę; 4 oy → U; 5 aw → U; 6 uw → ə; 9 ow → a), their consonants inserted or shifted (1 d → ž; 3 v → p; 4 t → š; 5 ∅ → k; 7 ∅ → p; 8 b → p; 10 ∅ → š) consequent to the transformations of grammatical category through the suffixation of +$\underline{ion}$.

(1)

1 divide	2 nation	3 conceive	4 permit
division	national	conception	permission
	nationalize	conceptacle	permissive

5 destroy	6 profound	7 presume
destruction	profundity	presumptuous
(in)destructible		

8 inscribe	9 morose	10 convene
inscription	morosity	convention

Students of English morphology and phonology have always known that words such as these, while preponderant in the English lexicon, are of foreign origin, and that the rules of word formation, adjustment, and allomorphy needed to generate them depend on special rubrics such as 'nonnative', 'Romance', 'French', or 'Latinate'. The morphophonology of these forms is especially fiendish since it combines the morphologies and phonologies of, often, three different languages: Latin, French, and English.

The derivational side of the English lexicon will be dominated by the rubric 'Latinate'. Much of the morphophonology, both adjustment and allomorphy, will be managed by this rubric as well. We can get a valuable perspective on the premises of Aronoff's approach to morphology by examining the generation of cognate vocabulary in the grammars of languages where this vocabulary and the processes associated with it are native. Cognates of the words of list (1) occur in all Romance languages; however, the morphophonemic variation that occurs in Spanish, Italian, and French is unremarkable when compared to that of Portuguese. See list (2).

(2) Portuguese cognates.

1 dividir	2 nação	3 conceber
divisão	nacional	concepção
divisional	nacionalizar	concepcional
4 permitir	5 destrói	6 profundo
permissão	destruição	profundidade
permissionário	destrutivo	
7 presumir	8 inscrever	9 moroso
presunção	inscrição	morosidade
10 convir		
convenção		
convencional		

Examination of the origin of the _i_ that appears in forms putatively derived from nouns: permissão$_N$ ⟶ permissionário$_{Adj-N}$ and the alternation between nonderived -ão [ãw] and derived -on- [on] such as convenção and convencional will reveal shortcomings in the word-based approach to morphophonology.[4]

Any principled theory of morphophonology will have to reconcile the morphophonemic variation attested in list (2) with the following phenomena. Portuguese nominals ending in -ão in their singular forms may have either -ãos [-ãws], -ões [-õys], or -ães [-ãys] as plural endings: irmão-irmãos, nação - nações, cão - cães. Derived words related to these indicate morphophonemic variation: irmão - irmanar ('brother' - 'to make a brother of'), nação - nacional ('nation' - 'national'), cão - canino ('dog' - 'canine'). It would be both ad hoc and complicated to generate the plurals and the derived forms from nonderived words as in (3). These arguments are so ad hoc and unnatural that they appear to be 'straw man' formulations designed to be torn to shreds, yet they are implicit in at least one[5] article on the generation of plurals in Portuguese and are imperative in Aronoff's theory of word formation.

Both the plurals and the morphologically derived forms related to singular nominals ending in -ão in Portuguese can be generated in a principled manner by basing one's rules on a dictionary entry which is not the simple, nonderived word, but which is an underlying form that is motivated by the stem which occurs in derived words. See (4).

At this point the phonology, both generalized and dialectal, takes over in readying these forms for their surface

(3) First generation: Ultra natural.

Paradigmatic → Plurals	Derivation → Noun → Adj.
irmão$_N$ + /z/ irmãos	irmão$_N$ + a$_{TV}$ + d + o ão → án / __ + a + irman+a+d+o irmanado
nação$_N$ + /z/ -ão$_1$ → õe / __ + /z/ nações	nação$_N$ + /al/$_{Adj}$ -ão$_1$ → ón / __ + /al/ naçõnal ∅ → /i/ / +strid __ on+al naciónal V → V̂ / __ /1/# nacionál
cão$_N$ + /z/ -ão$_2$ → ãe/ __ + /z/ -cães	cão$_N$ + /in/$_{Adj}$ + o -ão$_2$ → án+/__ +in+o cán+in+o V → V̂/CV# canino

manifestations. The morphophonemic nature of the Portuguese writing system is apparent in these generations.

These rules, with the exception of the morpholexical rule, will generate the plurals of the forms in question. See (5). Again, at this point the phonology will operate freely, with no need to refer to grammatical structure, on the forms in question.

On the other hand, these same bases combine freely with deriving suffixes and cause no morphophonemic alternation:

nas+sion$_N$ + al$_{Adj}$ +e k+an$_N$ + in$_{Adj}$ +o irm+an$_N$ + a$_{Vb}$

They are immediately reentered into the word stock. Stress assignment, the deletion of /e/ after /1/ etc. will be handled by morphophonemic rules in the obligatory, paradigmatic, part of the Portuguese morphological component. Scheme 2 exemplifies the lexical model of Scheme 1. In English the scheme would work as in Scheme 3.

The data that I have examined in this paper leads me to conclude that:

(1) Linguists dealing with morphology, phonology, and the lexicon must decide what they mean by statements such as 'each word may be entered in the dictionary as a fully specified separate item'.[6] When taken literally this dictum forces undue complication and haphazard behavior on the morphophonology. Besides this, it complicates the creative and obligatory sides unnecessarily. For example, in Portuguese nouns are

(4) Second generation: Principled natural.
----
nas+sion+e   k+an+e   irm+an+o

A morpholexical rule will neutralize these suffixes in nonderived singular forms:

$$\begin{bmatrix} + \text{(si)on+} \\ +\text{an+} \end{bmatrix} /e/+ \rightarrow /\text{an+o}/ \begin{bmatrix} -\text{fem} \\ -\text{pl} \\ -\text{derived} \end{bmatrix}$$

Morphophonemic rules (adjustment and allomorphy) will:

A. Assign stress to penult vowel:
   V → +stress / __ C_0^4 - C C_0^1 #
   nas+sián+o   k+án+o   irm+án+o

B. Nasalize vowels:

   V → +nasal / + __ $\begin{bmatrix} +\text{nasal} \\ +\text{anterior} \\ +\text{coronal} \end{bmatrix}$ + V$_{-\text{derived}}$

   nas+siá̃n+o   k+ã́n+o   irm+ã́n+o

C. Delete /n/:

   +nasal → ∅ $\begin{bmatrix} +\text{nasal} \\ +\text{voc} \end{bmatrix}$ __ +V

   nas+siã́+o   k+ã́+o   irm+ã́+o

D. Delete /i/[7]

   $\begin{bmatrix} +\text{voc} \\ +\text{high} \end{bmatrix}$ → ∅ / +(s)__ $\begin{bmatrix} +\text{voc} \\ +\text{nasal} \end{bmatrix}$

   nas+sã́+o

----

(5) Second generation: Plurals.
----
	nas+sion+e+z	k+an+e+z	irm+an+o+z
(A)	nas+sión+e+z	k+án+e+z	irm+án+o+z
(B)	nas+siṍn+e+z	k+ã́n+e+z	irm+ã́n+o+z
(C)	nas+siṍ+e+z	k+ã́+e+z	irm+ã́+o+z
(D)	nas+sṍ+e+z	*****	*****

Scheme 2. Portuguese morphology in action.

Dictionary Entry: nas+sion$_N$ + e nas+sion+al+e

```
        Inflection                Derivation
Sing.           Plural          WFR  N → Adj.
nas+sion+e+∅   nas+sion+e+z     nas+sion$_N$ + al$_{Adj}$ + e ...
```

MORPHOLEXICAL RULE
```
│ │            │ │
nas+sian+o     *****
│ │            │ │
```
MORPHOPHONEMIC RULES............Derived Entry

(A) Stress
    sing   plural   sing   plural
    nas+sián+o   nas+sión+e+z   nas+sion+ál+e   nas+sion+ál+e+z
(B) Nasalization
    nas+siãn+o   nas+siõn+e+z   *****   *****
(C) Deletion of /n/
    nas+siã+o   nas+siõ+e+z   *****   *****
(D) Deletion of /i/
    nas+sã+o   nas+sõ+e+z   *****   *****
(E) Deletion of /l/ / __+e+z
    *****   *****   *****   nas+sion+á+e+z
(F) Deletion of /e/ / /l/ __#
    *****   *****   nas+sion+ál   *****

Scheme 3. English morphology in action.

Dictionary Entry: nášən   nášənəl

```
Inflection                    Derivation

Sing       Plural             WFR  N → Adj

nášən+∅    nášən+z            nášən$_N$ + əl$_{Adj}$ ...
```

MORPHOPHONEMICS

1. Vowel shift /ä/ → /éy/ / ___ [-derived]⁸
   néyšə (z)
---

obligatorily inflected, they cannot surface without a
gender morpheme (traditionally the citation form is
-feminine), but in the word-based scheme they must be
de-inflected for the purpose of derivation, later they
are re-inflected in order to surface.
(2) The creative side of morphology (derivation) preserves
the underlying structure of words, whereas the paradigmatic side of morphology tends to obfuscate the
underlying form in its passage from the word stock to
the surface of the language. Within this scheme the
bulk of morphophonemic variation is, then, the result
of the lack of word forming processes rather than as
Aronoff would have it, the direct result of these processes.
(3) The only principled way of generating the pluralization of nominals and the morphophonemic alternation
that occurs between derived and nonderived forms in
Portuguese is from the stem that occurs in derived
forms. Rules A, B, and C are not limited to this
sector of the Portuguese lexicon: they are independently motivated, general, rules of Portuguese,
and they recapitulate the unique historical phonology
of the evolution of Portuguese from Latin.
(4) Using bases motivated in derived vocabulary as the
point of departure for morphological and phonological
operations satisfies and at the same time transcends
the strong naturalness condition. Surface manifestations continue to justify the base, yet the grammar
continues to be a principled account of linguistic
structure rather than a list.[9]

Even though English nominals have no apparent obligatory
inflection for gender and number, this approach to morphology
and morphophonemic variation is helpful in English as well.
The vowel and consonant alternation of list (1) can be generated more efficiently and naturally using the stem that
occurs in derived nominals as the base of operations.

NOTES

1. The MIT Press, 1976.
2. The abstract categorical input is the product of the
base component which we presume to be universal. It contains the derived strings of the deep structure (abstract
base markers). The first task of the grammar of any particular language is to convert universal categories (Noun, Verb,
etc.) into the specific units of that language. The ANALYSIS
of Noun in Romance indicates that nouns consist of stems together with gender and number morphemes. Further ANALYSIS
indicates that gender is either marked as ±feminine or is

idiomatic (unmarked) and number is ±plural. Once the grammatical categories are refined to their ultimate constituents, these ultimate constituents receive a phonological definition by the READJUSTMENT RULES using the DISTINCTIVE FEATURE MATRIX (the universal articulatory parameters of human speech). Then these phonologically specified, grammatically analyzed, morphosyntactic entities (words and affixes) will be entered into the WORD STOCK in a shape reflected by at least one surface manifestation. At this point items in the WORD STOCK may either (1) surface directly after passing through the PARADIGMATIC (inflectional) part of the morphology of the language where words receive the affix(es) which are determined by their syntactic environment (i.e. adjective-noun agreement in number and gender in Romance), whereupon they receive any necessary adjustment in the MORPHOPHONOLOGY of the specific language, after which they are ready for the PHONOLOGICAL COMPONENT which processes the articulatory parameters automatically, without recourse to grammatical information; or (2) they may serve as the base for the creative side of morphology, the DERIVATION of new words. In this section they receive additional suffixes which must be defined and specified in a section of the DICTIONARY ENTRIES and which transform the form class of preexisting words—at times occasioning segmental deletions or modifications. The products of the WORD FORMING RULES and any MORPHOPHONOLOGY exclusively contained in them are reentered into the WORD STOCK, either to be rederived upon or to be fitted into their syntactic environment by the PARADIGMATIC (inflectional) morphology with all necessary adjustments and allomorphies of the MORPHOPHONOLOGY (see Scheme 2). The PARADIGMATIC (inflectional) rules of MORPHOLOGY are automatic and obligatory, thus noncreative; whereas the DERIVATIONAL rules are optional, hence, creative. All rules which require the presence of structural (grammatical) features: word and morpheme boundaries, major class designations, syntactic environments, etc. are MORPHOPHONEMIC. PHONOLOGY, the grammar of articulation, operates independently.

3. Active utilization of grammatical rules by native speakers in their day-to-day linguistic activity is, at best, a moot point. The rules that linguists write describe real underlying patterns that enable human beings to learn their languages; but human beings, once they have learned their language, have ways of circumventing their grammar, especially when they process utterances. Grammar gets the native out of scrapes.

4. In the Romance languages where /i/ occurs in all forms, i.e. Spanish <u>división</u>, <u>nación</u>, <u>concepción</u>, <u>destrucción</u>, etc. (cf. French and Italian) there is no alternation of vowels and consonants (French word-final vowel nasalization and the

deletion of nasal consonants is phonological rather than morphophonemic) the base for derivation is not problematic as there is no morphophonemic variation.

5. John Lipski, 'The surface structure of Portuguese and other things', Linguistics 111.67-82.

6. There is ample evidence in Aronoff's work that he is not terribly sure what he means (98): '... rules of allomorphy ... cannot introduce segments which are not otherwise motivated by underlying phonological segments of the language. This of course makes them very different from rules of the phonology'. But (112): 'The central import of allomorphy rules is for the phonology ... making predictions about the range of material that can be covered by rules of phonology ...' AND (113): 'We are not denying the validity of the English main stress rule, because of its baroque complexity. Phonological rules may be as baroque as they wish to be, but rules of allomorphy, as defined, will always precede the rules of phonology'. The whole point of the natural constraints of lexical representation and the incorporation of morphology as a separate component of the grammar of a language is to simplify and define phonology. Aronoff's inconsistency concerning the relationship of morphology and phonology will motivate a second part to this paper, an examination of English morphophonology in the light of the premises advocated here.

7. Apparent exceptions to this rule are words such as pião 'top', Sião 'Zion', ocasião 'ocasion', tabelião 'record keeper', and rebelião 'rebellion'. The /i/ remains in these forms because their underlying structure is not that described in rule D; it is /pi+on+e/, /#sion+e#/, /okazi+on+e/, /tabeli+an+e/, and /r̃ebeli+on+e/.

8. There is a single rule of vowel shift to handle all the alternations of list (1). This rule departs from the stem which occurs in derived forms and generates the tense vowels of nonderived forms:

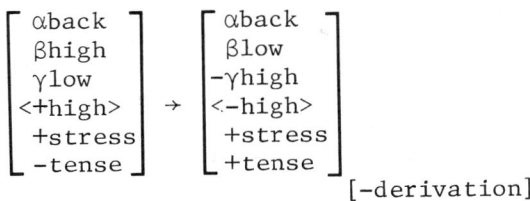

[-derivation]

9. During the session at which this paper was presented, Virginia Jellech reminded us that the principle advocated here is the same used for entries in Latin and Greek dictionaries. Citation forms are not nominative singular nor infinitive forms; they are, rather, forms motivated by morphophonemic variation.

THE BILINGUAL LEXICON AND LINGUISTIC INNOVATION

CHARLES ELERICK
University of Texas at El Paso

    In some respects, the internalized grammar of the bilingual is different in kind from that of the monolingual. One difference can be found in the nature of the bilingual's lexicon. The lexicon of the bilingual, in addition to entries that are proper to each of the two languages he speaks, includes certain union entries. By 'union entry' I mean the abstract representation that simultaneously underlies coordinate items in both languages of the bilingual which are phonologically and otherwise similar to such an extent that the bilingual could not fail to notice that the two language-specific manifestations were the 'same word'. These union entries must be very extensive in the case of the English/Spanish bilingual in view of the existence of hundreds, even thousands, of paired items such as 'decide'/<u>decidir</u>, 'battle'/<u>batalla</u>, and 'fabulous'/<u>fabuloso</u>. While there are interesting questions concerning the nature of the interrelationships between Spanish and English semantic ranges and Spanish and English syntactic classification, my discussion of lexical interaction will be limited to matters of phonology.
    I assume that a union lexical entry includes a single underlying phonological representation. I further assume that these union phonological representations are linked to their respective manifestations by parallel sets of English and Spanish phonological rules. Both of these sets of rules are somewhat special in that they include rules that would not be part of a monolingual grammar of either English or Spanish. The occurrence of special rules in the phonological component results from the somewhat greater abstractness of underlying representation that is necessary in an intersection grammar.

Below are additional pairs of items of Spanish and English which can be assumed to correspond to a single union entry in the lexicon of the bilingual. Associated with each pair, represented in standard orthography, is the underlying phonological form that I posit as common to both manifestations. In some items there are minor exceptions that must be noted and this information would be included as part of the entry as well.

(1) 'human'/humano /hūmano+/
(2) 'hymn'/himno   /himno+/
(3) 'idiot'/idiota /idiota+/
(4) 'desert'/desierto /dezerto+/
(5) 'east'/este   /Este+/
(6) 'debate'/debate /dEbAte+/
(7) 'legal'/legal   /lEgal+/
(8) 'fine'/fino   /fIno+/
(9) 'brief'/breve   /brEve+/
(10) 'orthography'/ortografía /orθografia+/
(11) 'stranger'/estranjero /strAnγero+/
(12) 'passion'/pasión /pasyon+/
(13) 'fiber'/fibra   /fIbra+/
(14) 'theatre'/teatro /θEatro+/

The first thing that the observer should notice about these underlying representations is that they employ segmental entities that betoken certain contrasts that are commonly assumed for either Spanish or English but here are used as a larger conjoined set. It would be inappropriate, for example, to posit for Spanish underlying forms with /h/, /v/, /θ/, /z/ or any of a class of tense vowels that undergo vowel shift in English derivations, and which are represented here by upper case letters. On the other hand, dipthongizing syllabic nuclei such as those evident in the alternation in Spanish tener/tiene and here in desierto is a phenomenon unknown in English. There are, in addition, some underlying segments in a union phonological grammar that are not properly a part of either language and which would occur only in the grammar of a bilingual. An example of such a segment is /γ/, which occurs here in /strAnγero+/.

Following are some exemplary derivations that will demonstrate more clearly the relationships that obtain between the Spanish and English items, their union representations and the rules that link each underlying representation to its two manifestations. All the rules that are illustrated by the forms in the exemplary derivations are supported by a much larger sample of Spanish/English pairs. For the purpose of this paper I have informally characterized each rule. Rules that would not be part of a monolingual grammar of English or Spanish are designated as special (spec.). There is much low level phonetic detail that is not specified by the rules. These details include the aspiration of English stops, the nasalization of vowels before nasals, the dental vs. alveolar articulation of Spanish and English [+ant,+cor] segments respectively, the variation in English and Spanish nonnasal sonorants, etc. This phonetic detail is omitted as not essential to the thrust of this paper.

It should be noted that stress assignment is handled here in a highly abbreviated fashion. I have simply assigned stress at the appropriate point in the derivations and attributed this to the operation of the stress cycle. Note also that the tense vowels that undergo vowel shift in English derivations are otherwise equivalent to the corresponding tense vowel. Therefore, in the Spanish derivations they are handled as the latter and are conventionally represented as ē, etc. after the application of the Spanish vowel-tensing rule.

'human'/humano

/hūmano+/
hūman (final V del.)
  (spec.)
húmàn (stress cycle)
hyūmàn (y insertion)
hyūmn̩ (syllable reduction)

/hūmano+/
ūmano (h deletion)
  (spec.)
ūmáno (stress cycle)
ūmā́nō (vowel tensing)

'idiot'/idiota

/idiota+/
idiot (final V del.)
  (spec.)
ídiòt (stress cycle)
ídīòt (vowel tensing)
ídīət (vowel reduction)

/idiota+/
idióta (stress cycle)
iðióta (vcd. stop lenition)
iðyóta (i→y)
īðyōtā́ (vowel tensing)

'legal'/legal

/lEgal+/
lEgal (stress cycle)
lígal (vowel shift)
lígl̩ (syllable reduction)

/lEgal+/
lEgál (stress cycle)
lēgā́l (vowel tensing)

'desert'/desierto

/dezerto+/
dezert (final vowel deletion) (spec.)
dézèrt (stress cycle)
dézr̩t (syllable reduction)

/dezerto+/
dezérto (stress cycle)
dezyérto (dipthongization)
desyérto (fric. devoicing)
dēsyērtō (vowel tensing)

'brief'/<u>breve</u>

/brEve+/
- brEv (final V del.) (spec.)
- brEv (stress cycle)
- brív (vowel shift)
- brĭf (obstruent devoicing)

/brĘve+/
- brĘve (stress cycle)
- brēvē (vowel tensing)
- brēβē (v→β) (spec.)

'orthography'/<u>ortografía</u>

/orθografia+/
- orθografi (final vowel deletion) (spec.)
- orθografì (stress cycle)
- orθágrafì (o→a)
- orθágrəfì (vowel reduction)
- orθágrəfī́ (word final vowel tensing)

/orθografia+/
- òrθografía (stress cycle)
- òrtografía (θ→t) (spec.)
- ōrtōgrāfīā (vowel tensing)

'stranger'/<u>estranjero</u>

/strAnγero+/
- strAnγer (final V del.) (spec.)
- strÁnγèr (stress cycle)
- strḗnγèr (vowel shift)
- strḗnjèr (γ→j) (spec.)
- strḗnjr̩ (syllable reduction)

/strAnγero+/
- strAnγéro (stress cycle)
- estrAnγéro (epenthesis)
- estrAŋγéro (nasal assim.)
- estrAŋxéro (fric. devoicing)
- ēstrāŋxḗrō (vowel tensing)

'passion'/<u>pasión</u>

/pasyon+/
- pásyòn (stress cycle)
- pǽsyòn (a→æ) (spec.)
- pǽšòn (sy→š) (spec.)
- pǽšn̩ (syllable reduction)

/pasyon+/
- pasyón (stress cycle)
- pāsyṓn (vowel tensing)

The bilingual's initial motivation for the internalization of union lexical entries is the apparent economy that can be gained by employing such a device. However, the actual result of having union entries is the complication of the grammar as a whole. This complication is first evident in the increased inventory of underlying segments, differentiated by either articulatory or special status features. The additional rules that must be posited to reconcile the underlying union forms constitute additional complication.

The bilingual is then confronted with a dilemma: it is simply impossible for him--that is, his subconscious grammar internalization mechanism--to overlook the systematic relationships that obtain between immense numbers of Spanish and English items. At the same time, the result of this lexical rapprochement is a significant increase in the complication of his grammar and the derivational complexity with respect to individual items.

Economy is highly valued, but comprehensive economy cannot be achieved with lexical representations which along with a significantly complicated phonological component specify standard English and standard Spanish manifestations. The result is grammar simplification, and this simplification takes place at the expense of the standard forms.

To illustrate the effect and significance of the pressure for simplification that bears on the bilingual grammar, seven innovative forms used by some speakers of Spanish in the United States will be discussed. These forms are previewed below and correspond to standard English, standard Spanish, and innovative Spanish from left to right respectively.

'telephone'	teléfono	telefón
'population'	población	populación
'gasoline'	gasolina	gasolín
'caramel'	caramelo	carmelo
'ancestor'	ansestro	ansestor
'alcohol'	alcohol	alcajol
'champion'	campeón	champión

On the ensuing pages I will offer a discussion of these items within the following format. First, the union phonological representation that underlies both the standard forms along with the respective surface derivations will be presented. Then, the standard English and innovative Spanish form will be similarly presented, with their underlying representation and respective derivations. On the basis of observable contrasts in lexical and derivational complexity, certain conclusions regarding innovation in bilingual grammars will then be advanced.

$$\begin{array}{ll} & \text{'telephone'/teléfono} \\ \text{/telefōno+/} & \text{/telefōno+/} \\ \quad \text{telefōn (final V del.)} & \quad \text{teléfōno (minor stress} \\ \quad \text{télefōn (stress cycle)} & \quad \text{rule)} \\ \quad \text{télǝfōn (vowel reduction)} & \quad \text{tēlēfōnō (V. tensing)} \end{array}$$

'telephone'/telefón
/telefōn+/   /telefōn+/
 télefǭn (stress cycle)   telefṓn (stress cycle)
 télǝfōn (vowel reduc-   tēlēfōn (V. tensing)
   tion)

The substitution of telefón by a bilingual brings about simplification in his lexicon and in the derivation of surface forms in both languages. In addition to shortening the lexical form by one segment, special status information specifying the irregular stressing of the standard form is unnecessary. Perhaps it should be made clear that the stressing of the last syllable in telefón is completely regular since the word-final nasal is a lexical rather than grammatical formative segment. The simplification in the English derivation is easily observable but not so in the Spanish derivation. I consider that the fact that it is unnecessary to refer to a minor stress rule in the derivation amounts to a simplification.

'population'/población
/popūlAsyon+/   /popūlAsyon+/
 pòpūlÁsyon (stress   poplAsyon (minor rule)
   cycle)   poblAsyón (minor rule)
 pòpyūlÁsyon (y inser-   poblAsyón (stress
   tion)   cycle)
 pòpyūlḗsyon (vowel   pōblāsyṓn (V. tensing)
   shift)
 pàpyūlḗsyon (o→a)
 pàpyūlḗšon (sy→š)
   (spec.)
 pàpyūlḗšn̩ (syllable
   reduction)

'population'/población
/popūlAsyon+/   /popūlAsyon+/
 pòpūlÁsyon (stress   pòpūlAsyṓn (stress
   cycle)   cycle)
 pòpyūlÁsyon (y inser-   pōpūlāsyṓn (V. tens-
   tion)   ing)
 pòpyūlḗsyon (vowel
   shift)
 pàpyūlḗsyon (o→a)
 pàpyūlḗšon (sy→š)
   (spec.)
 pàpyūlḗšn̩ (syllable
   reduction)

The innovation of populación has the effect of simplifying the union phonological entry and the Spanish derivation. The lexical form is relieved of two segment specific special status indicators. One of these marks /ū/ for deletion and another marks the second /p/ for voicing. The effect of the innovative union lexical form on the Spanish derivation is substantial and obvious.

              'gasoline'/gasolina
/gasolīna+/   /gasolīna+/
  gasolīn (final V dele-   gasolīna (stress
    tion) (spec.)   cycle)
  gásolīn (stress cycle)   gāsōlīnā (vowel
  gásəlīn (vowel reduc-   tensing)
    tion)
  gǽsəlīn (a→æ)(spec.)

              'gasoline'/gasolín
/gasolín+/   /gasolín+/
  gásolīn (stress cycle)   gasolín (stress cycle)
  gásəlīn (vowel reduc-   gāsōlín (vowel tensing)
    tion)
  gǽsəlīn (a→æ) (spec.)

By substituting gasolín for gasolina the bilingual enjoys a real though minor saving in his lexicon and one complication, also relatively minor, in the sequence of rules that specify the English manifestation.

              'caramel'/caramelo
/karamelo+/   /karamelo+/
  karamel (final V dele-   karamélo (stress cycle)
    tion)   kārāmēlō (vowel
  karmel (minor rule)   tensing)
    (spec.)
  kármèl (stress cycle)
  kɔ́rmèl (a→ɔ)
  kɔ́rmì (syllable reduc-
    tion)

              'caramel'/carmelo
/karmelo+/   /karmelo+/
  karmel (final V dele-   karmélo (stress cycle)
    tion) (spec.)   kārmēlō (vowel
  kármèl (stress cycle)   tensing)
  kɔ́rmèl (a→ɔ)
  kɔ́rmì (syllable reduc-
    tion)

The replacement of the underlying form /karamelo+/ with /karmelo+/ involves important simplification in that no special status information relating to the syncopation of the medial syllable in the English manifestation is necessary in the innovative form. The English derivation is also correspondingly simplified.

                        'ancestor'/ansestro

/ansestro+/   /ansestro+/
  ansestr (final V dele-   anséstro (stress cycle)
    tion) (spec.)   ānsēstrō (vowel
  ansestr̩ (syllabifi-   tensing)
    cation)
  ánsestr̩ (stress cycle)
  ǽnsestr̩ (a→æ) (spec.)

                        'ancestor'/ansestor

/ansestor+/   /ansestor+/
  ánsestòr (stress   ansestór (stress
    cycle)   cycle)
  ǽnsestòr (a→æ) (spec.)   ānsēstōr (vowel
  ǽnsestr̩ (syllable   tensing)
    reduction)

For this pair, the innovative lexical representation is not demonstrably simpler than that it replaces. The new form does, however, occasion a simpler English derivation.

                      'alcohol'/alcohol

/alkohol+/   /alkohol+/
  álkohòl (stress cycle)   alkool (h deletion)
  álkəhòl (vowel reduc-   alkol (ident. V dele-
    tion)   tion)
  ǽlkəhòl (a→æ) (spec.)   alkól (stress cycle)
  ǽlkəhɔ̀l (o→ɔ)

                      'alcohol'/alcajol

/alkaxol+/   /alkaxol+/
  alkahol (x→h) (spec.)   alkaxól (stress cycle)
  álkahòl (stress cycle)   ālkāxōl (vowel
  álkəhòl (vowel reduc-   tensing)
    tion)
  ǽlkəhòl (a→æ) (spec.)
  ǽlkəhɔ̀l (o→ɔ)

As is the case in the preceding example, both the innovative representation and the representation it supersedes are equally complex. Here the Spanish derivation is simplified while the English derivation is complicated to an approximately equal extent.

                        'champion'/campeón
/kampEon+/   /kampEon+/
  kámpEòn (stress cycle)   kampEón (stress cycle)
  kámpīòn (vowel tensing)   kāmpēón (vowel
  kámpīn̥ (syllable reduc-   tensing)
    tion)
  čámpīn̥ (minor rule)
    (spec.)
  čǽmpīn̥ (a→æ) (spec.)

                        'champion'/champión
/čampion+/   /čampion+/
  čámpiòn (stress cycle)   čampión (stress cycle)
  čámpīòn (vowel tens-   čampyón (i→y)
    ing)   čāmpyón (vowel
  čámpīn̥ (syllable reduc-   tensing)
    tion)
  čǽmpīn̥ (a→æ) (spec.)

The restructuring of the lexicon through the replacement of /kampEon+/ by /campion+/ results in substantial simplification in the lexicon and some simplification in the English derivation. The English derivational simplification is, however, approximately matched by complication in the Spanish derivation, leaving as the net gain in economy that of the lexicon. The lexical simplification is more radical than might be evident at first glance, involving the elimination of the inclusion of /k/ in a k→č minor rule and the replacement of the more complex /E/ by /i/.

In this paper I have developed the essentials of a formal framework and a discovery procedure based on this framework and have employed both in an attempt to understand certain aspects of linguistic change in a language contact situation. In this regard I consider the concept of the union lexical entry and the use of contrastive derivations that proceed from alternate lexical representations to be important.

On the basis of this study the following general observations and tentative conclusions can be drawn. The innovative Spanish forms are, of course, more like their English counterparts than the forms they replace. What is perhaps noteworthy is the fact that the general effect of the greater similarity of the surface form and the innovative lexical form that underlies the partially new pair is the simplification of the English derivation. This is true in five of the seven cases inspected here. I have no explanation for the fact but am certain that it has some significance. It will bear further study.

Secondly, it would seem obvious from the data and analyses presented here that there is a definite relationship between the pressure for grammatical change that takes place in a monolingual setting and the pressures that bring about the innovation of nonstandard forms in a bilingual's grammar and hence in a bilingual community. It would follow then, that the bilingual community is likely to be an especially good place for those interested in language change to look for examples of linguistic systems in flux. It is also motivation, for those who are not so inclined, to view the innovation of nonstandard forms in a bilingual community as a very natural development and not the result of some perversity.

The most important conclusion that can be drawn from this paper should be the most obvious but is probably not. This paper reaffirms that languages in contact are systems in contact. The interaction between languages in contact situations is between these systems and not between items, as such. This is tantamount to repeating the now standard dictum of modern linguistics, that linguistic change is grammatical change and that the change that is observable in the forms of the language is the manifestation of grammatical change.

REFERENCES

Bowen, Donald J. 1975. Adaptation of English borrowing. In: El lenguaje de los Chicanos. Edited by Eduardo Hernández-Chávez, Andrew D. Cohen, and Anthony F. Beltramo. Arlington, Va.: Center for Applied Linguistics.

Chomsky, N., and Morris Halle. 1968. The sound pattern of English. New York: Harper and Row.

King, Robert D. 1969. Historical linguistics and generative grammar. Englewood Cliffs, N.J.: Prentice-Hall.

Teshner, Richard V. 1972. Anglicisms in Spanish: A cross-referenced guide to previous findings, together with English lexical influence on Chicago Mexican Spanish. Unpublished dissertation, University of Wisconsin, Madison.

INDIGENISMS IN MEXICAN SPANISH:
A SOCIOLINGUISTIC APPROACH

LEE ANN GRACE
State University College at Buffalo

Throughout our investigation of the influence of bilingualism on sixteenth-century Mexican Spanish, we have focused on the linguistic production of different social groups, particularly on their use of indigenisms. Unlike phonetic features, these lexical borrowings from the Indian languages can be readily identified in the written texts upon which historical studies must rely. In view of this methodological advantage as well as the general preponderance of lexical over nonlexical borrowing,[1] it is not surprising that loanword studies and dictionaries of indigenisms have predominated among the works on language contact in Spanish America. For the most part, however, these works provide mere lists of words, definitions, and perhaps etymologies, while almost uniformly ignoring the 'process' of linguistic change and the social context in which the contact occurred--precisely the aspects of the linguistic situation in colonial Mexico which we shall attempt to clarify.

While it is apparent that the contact between Nahuatl and Spanish initiated some significant changes in the lexicon of Mexican Spanish, it is rather less obvious how these changes took place.

We know, of course, that the Spaniards dealt linguistically with the reality of New Spain in a number of ways. Among these, perhaps the simplest was extending the meaning of a Spanish word to denote something similar in America. Thus, the conquerors referred to the natives' flat corn bread as tortillas (rather than tlaxcalli) and called turkeys gallinas de la tierra, gallos de papada, or pavas (rather than huexolotl). Still another option available to the Spaniards was the use of indigenisms from the Antilles, many of which

were already integrated into American Spanish by the early
1520s, when Mexico was conquered. In fact Antillean maíz,
canoa, and cacique were so thoroughly assimilated by the
time Cortés arrived in Mexico that the corresponding Nahuatl
terms tlaolli, acalli, and tlatoqui almost never occur, except by way of citing the Aztec equivalent. By far the most
frequent solution, however, was the borrowing of Nahuatl
terms. But these three processes were by no means mutually
exclusive, and their concurrent functioning often resulted
in competition between Nahuatlisms, Antilleanisms, and Spanish terms.

Rivalry of this sort is an important feature of historical
Hispanic linguistics, in that it reflects the process of linguistic change. By tracing the course of specific rival
terms from the sixteenth century to the present, we have attempted to clarify their changing status and to exemplify
some of the ways in which the competition between terms was
resolved.

Indications of the eventual outcome of some rivalry situations can be observed already in the second half of the sixteenth century. We have studied prose works[2] written in
Spanish by eleven authors from this period, authors who
represent various social and linguistic categories found in
colonial Mexico (bilingual native Spaniards: Fray Bernardino
de Sahagún, Fray Diego Durán, and Fray Domingo de la Anunci-
ación; mestizos: Juan Bautista Pomar and Diego Muñoz Camargo; criollos: Juan Suárez de Peralta, Fray Juan Bautista,
and Fray Agustín Dávila Padilla; and monolingual native
Spaniards: Viceroy Luis de Velasco I, Francisco Cervantes
Salazar, and Dr. Juan de Cárdenas).[3] Additional historical
perspective has been gleaned from Peter Boyd-Bowman's Léxico
hispanoamericano del siglo XVI;[4] from the data collected by
Boyd-Bowman for forthcoming volumes on the seventeenth and
eighteenth centuries;[5] and from Juan Lope Blanch's El léxico
indígena en el español de México,[6] which examines the indigenisms (primarily Nahuatlisms) used today in Mexico City.
The current status of certain items was further checked, on
an informal basis, with a Mexican informant.

It is clear that the chances of an Aztec item becoming
integrated into Spanish varied greatly. In some rare cases
the Nahuatl borrowing (e.g. cacao) was accepted at once as
the sole means of expressing the referent. In other instances the Nahuatlism flourished in the early colonial
period, only to disappear later. This occurred with a number of items like macehual 'a vassal, a commoner in the
social hierarchy of the Indians'. When the referent vanished,
so did the term. Sometimes, however, despite the passing of
the original referent from the scene, the indigenism survived by virtue of its meaning having been extended to denote something else. Mitote, for example, at the time of the

Conquest referred to the Aztecs' ceremonial dances; while in modern Mexico the term lives on in popular speech as an alternate for the more general _fiesta_ on the one hand, and for _pleito_ 'dispute' or _alboroto_ 'disturbance' on the other.[7] In still other instances a non-Nahuatl expression predominated in the years following the Conquest, but was eventually replaced by the indigenous Mexican term. Such was the result of the rivalry between Nahuatl _chile_ and Antillean _ají_, both referring to hot peppers.

Boyd-Bowman notes in the introduction to his _Léxico hispanoamericano del siglo XVI_ that _ají_ alone is encountered in documents written during the first twenty years after the Conquest and continues to be preferred over _chile_ for much of the century.[8] In the authors we have studied from 1550 to 1600, the competition of terms is apparent, but a trend toward favoring _chile_ is observed.[9] Sahagún alternates between _chile_ and _ají_ throughout the twelve books of his _Historia_, but the Nahuatlism occurs approximately twice for every occurrence of the Antilleanism. In Durán the preference for _chile_ is even more intense (about four to one). Moreover, authors such as _Cárdenas_ and Fray Juan Bautista, who were writing at the very end of the century, appear to use _chile_ to the exclusion of _ají_. The decline of the Antillean term is also borne out by the seventeenth-century entries in the volume of Boyd-Bowman's _Léxico_ which is currently in press. Occurrences of _chile_ in Mexican documents outnumber those of _ají_ in a ratio of two to one. By the eighteenth century _ají_ is not encountered at all in the Mexican sources used by Boyd-Bowman, and today in Mexico _chile_ has completely overshadowed the Antilleanism.

A somewhat more complex case of rivalry involves the Nahuatlisms _nochtli_ 'prickly pear' and _nopal_ 'cactus which produces prickly pears' and the corresponding Antilleanisms _tuna_ and _tunal_. _Tuna_ apparently had very little competition from _nochtli_, which has not survived. In fact, we found only three instances of _nochtli_ in the works of the eleven sixteenth-century writers studied and none at all in Boyd-Bowman's _Léxico_ (sixteenth, seventeenth, and eighteenth centuries). Moreover, those who have traveled in Mexico are aware that the fruit is still called by the Antillean name, _tuna_. The situation with _tunal_ and _nopal_, however, is quite different. The broader spread of _tunal_ among the authors investigated in the second half of the sixteenth century, as well as the larger number of Mexican entries in Boyd-Bowman's _Léxico_, suggest that _tunal_ dominated over _nopal_ throughout the 1500s, though it appears that _nopal_ was beginning to gain ground toward the end of the century.[10] The following two hundred years yield further examples of _nopal_ (two for each century in Boyd-Bowman's data), but the appearance of the derived term _nopalera_ (once in the seventeenth century, three times in the eighteenth) is even stronger evidence of the spread and integration of the Nahuatlism. Still, tunal did not die out. Instead, it continued to coexist with nopal, as is apparent from the four eighteenth-century examples included in Boyd-Bowman's data. Today, however, Lope Blanch tells us that nopal is the generally known name for the plant,[11] a fact which our informant confirmed.[12]

Though up to this point we have directed our attention to rivalry between Antilleanisms and Nahuatlisms, it should be stressed that Nahuatlisms also competed with Hispanic terms. A classic example of this sort of rivalry is that of petate and estera. The sixteenth-century authors in our study who have occasion to speak of these reed mats use both terms, though Spanish estera retains a slight edge in all but Sahagún, who prefers petate about three to one. Without a similar extensive study of authors from each of the other chronological periods, it is more difficult to evaluate the relative usage of rival terms when Spanish items are involved, since Boyd-Bowman's Léxico tends to deal less with common Spanish terms than with items which are typically American. Nevertheless, it is apparent that petate (cited by Boyd-Bowman for the first time in 1532) was quickly assimilated, giving rise to derived forms such as petatillo as early as the mid 1500s. Though the Nahuatlism seems to occur more frequently than estera throughout the sixteenth, seventeenth, and eighteenth centuries, today the preference for petate has become generalized.[13] Furthermore, Lope Blanch comments extensively upon the vitality shown by this particular Nahuatlism, citing such derived terms as petateada, petatearse, and petatero, as well as popular sayings such as liar el petate, meaning 'to die'.[14]

It should, however, be noted that the indigenism did not always prevail so forcefully, as witnessed by the case of Nahuatl tianguez[15] vs. Spanish mercado. Though Sahagún favors the Aztec term over the Hispanic one, he is unique among the eleven sixteenth-century authors we studied. Moreover, there is no indication in any subsequent period of either term's definitively overtaking the other. This, nevertheless, should not be construed as a sign of exact equivalence or interchangeability; rather, the tianguez is ordinarily viewed as a type of mercado. Today, though both tianguis (modern spelling) and mercado continue to function in the Spanish of Mexico, they have become semantically specialized. That is, tianguis denotes specifically an open-air Indian market, while mercado refers to a market of any other kind.

The foregoing examples represent but a few of the most salient types of competition among terms in Mexican Spanish. We have seen that the penetration of most indigenous items into the Spanish of New Spain did not occur instantly, nor did the indigenisms become integrated at the same pace. In some cases the rivalry has been resolved in favor of one term or the other (as with chile and tuna); while in others, two or more terms continue to exist, though usually with some specialization of meaning (such as tianguis and mercado).

Our sixteenth-century data suggest that the mestizo may have played a significant role in the resolution or perpetuation of such rivalry situations. Indeed, though Pomar and Muñoz Camargo share many characteristics which set them apart from writers of the other social classes studied,[16] these mestizo authors display marked and consistent differences in their choices among competing terms.

For example, while Pomar employs either Spanish choza or the Antilleanism bohío for 'hut', Muñoz Camargo uses Nahuatl xacal. In speaking of the Indian ceremonial dances, Pomar limits himself to areito, a term originating in the Antilles, whereas his fellow mestizo avails himself of the native Aztec term mitote. Maguey fiber is ixtli, a Nahuatlism, for Muñoz Camargo, but nequén, an Antilleanism,[17] for Pomar. The prickly-pear is referred to by Pomar as tuna, which is the Antillean term, but Muñoz Camargo uses tuna only as a means of defining the Nahuatl word nochtli.

In addition, Pomar insists upon the Antillean term ají to speak of the hot peppers so common in indigenous cooking, rather than using Nahuatl chile, which, as we have seen, was already beginning to replace ají. Unfortunately, since Muñoz Camargo does not mention this referent in his work, we have no point of comparison.

It would be logical to suppose that the attitudes of these mestizo authors toward the languages in contact affected the number of loans taken from one language or the other. Though we have no systematic way of measuring such attitudes, occasional remarks by the authors provide us with attitudinal clues. The information is spotty, but in the case of the mestizos it does shed considerable light on their linguistic behavior.

Pomar repeatedly identifies with his Spanish heritage and the Spanish language as opposed to his Indian ancestry and Nahuatl: 'piedras preciosas, que ellos llamaban teoxihuitl y nosotros turquesas' (p. 10);[18] 'un licor de un árbol que llamaban olli, de que hacían las pelotas con que jugaban y nosotros lo llamamos batey, que es lengua de las islas de Santo Domingo' (p. 12); 'cuilón, que quiere decir puto en nuestra lengua' (p. 31). This identification with the dominant group may explain to some extent Pomar's preference for Spanish or Antillean terms where a Nahuatlism might be expected. In fact, Pomar could represent a tendency among some mestizos to overcompensate in a period when they were much maligned.[19]

Muñoz Camargo, on the other hand, identifies with his Hispanic heritage in cultural and historical terms, but we find no overt linguistic identification: 'los llaman huipilli y los Españoles llaman camisas' (p. 9);[20] 'Este armado caballero ... daba grandes presentes, a manera de propinas, como cuando se doctoran nuestros letrados' (p. 46); 'Aposentados ... los nuestros en los Palacios de Xicotencatl' (p. 189); 'se decía ... que los nuestros eran dioses' (p. 190).

The explanation of these divergent linguistic attitudes may be found in the biographies of the two authors. In the case of Muñoz Camargo, the evidence clearly indicates that he maintained positive ties with both branches of his family tree,[21] which perhaps enabled him to accept his double linguistic heritage. Pomar, on the other hand, apparently resorted to his indigenous ancestry only when it was to his advantage.[22] He evidently wished to identify with the prestige group and, in order to do so, availed himself of all the means at his disposal, including lexical choice.

Based on present-day use of indigenisms in Mexico, it would seem that the Muñoz Camargos prevailed. However, the contrast between the two authors provides insights into the dynamics of change and the role attitudes may play in this change.

NOTES

1. As Uriel Weinreich (1968:56) points out in Languages in Contact (The Hague: Mouton), 'the vocabulary of a language ... is beyond question the domain of borrowing par excellence'.

2. These were restricted to letters, historical works, training manuals for priests and friars, and practical treatises on several subjects, such as medicine, in order to offset as much as possible the artificiality of written language. Though we had available to us documents which reflect more accurately the speech of the colonists, the sociolinguistic nature of the larger study of which the data in this paper are a part required biographical background which simply could not be retrieved from such documents. (See Lee Ann Grace, 'The effect of bilingualism on sixteenth-century Mexican Spanish', unpublished dissertation, SUNY at Buffalo, 1976, particularly pp. 7-15.)

3. Unfortunately we were unable to identify a reliable source written in Spanish by an Indian, which would have completed the social spectrum. We intended to use Fernando Alva Ixtlixóchitl, but there is considerable disagreement among scholars regarding the purity of his blood; and though Fernando Alvarado Tezoxómoc appears to have been a full-blooded Indian, the date of his Crónica Mexicana is uncertain. See Ángel María Garibay Kintana, Historia de la

literatura náhuatl, II (Mexico: Porrúa, 1954), pp. 308, 301.
4. London: Tamesis, 1971.
5. The seventeenth-century volume is currently in press at Tamesis. However, we consulted the raw data as it stood in June 1976; thus the figures we cite may be at variance with what appears in final published form.
6. Mexico: El Colegio de México, 1969.
7. Lope Blanch, p. 47.
8. P. xiii.
9. Though the mestizo Pomar uses only ají, this appears to be part of his overall preference for Antillean and Spanish terms. We can make no comparison with the behavior of our other mestizo writer, however; because, unfortunately, the referent does not occur in his work.
10. Boyd-Bowman cites nopal first in Mexico City in 1594. Moreover, Cárdenas and Dávila Padilla, who wrote in the very last years of the sixteenth century, employ nopal quite naturally, without explanation or definition.
11. Lope Blanch, p. 45.
12. Her only guess at what tunal might be was obviously based on the derivational characteristics of Spanish: 'a place where there are a lot of tunas'. When asked if tuna or tunal could ever refer to the cactus itself, she insisted that nopal is the cactus.
13. Lope Blanch, p. 48. In fact, our informant did not even recognize the word estera.
14. Lope Blanch, p. 39.
15. This is one of the more frequent sixteenth-century variant spellings of modern tianguis.
16. For example, the mestizos show a strong preference for forms which have not been adapted to Spanish phonology and morphology. Moreover, they provide the majority of loan translations and hybrid loans encountered in the works we studied.
17. In spite of its supposed Mayan origin, the word nequén is usually considered an Antilleanism because the Spaniards almost certainly learned it in the Antilles.
18. We quote from Joaquín García Icazbalceta's edition of Pomar's Relación de Tezcoco in Nueva colección de documentos para la historia de México, II (Mexico, 1891).
19. According to Magnus Mörner and Charles Gibson in 'Diego Muñoz Camargo and the segregation policy of the Spanish crown', HAHR, 42 (1962), 558-569; cf. p. 560, the terms vagrant and mestizo had become almost synonymous. By the end of the sixteenth century 'even a person of some distinction, who in earlier times would have passed as a "Spaniard", might now, to his detriment, be ranked according to his origin as a mestizo' under the growing caste system (p. 562).

20. We quote from Alfredo Chavero's edition of Muñoz Carmargo's <u>Historia de Tlaxcala</u> (Mexico, 1892).

21. As the son of a conquistador, his ties with his Spanish background are evident, and there are numerous indications of his link to the indigenous side. Most notably, on a trip to Spain in 1584-85 he served as interpreter for a group of prominent Tlaxcalan Indians, was later honored by the Indian municipal council, and was named legal representative and financial manager for the community.

22. Pomar's mother was the illegitimate daughter of Nezahualpilli, the last Texcocan king. At the time of writing his <u>Relación</u>, Pomar is reported to have aspired to the government of the city of Texcoco and the patrimony his royal ancestors had left to others. Such aspirations were possible since the election of a successor to the Texcocan throne depended on merit rather than legitimacy. Pomar based his claim of merit on his being the son of a Spaniard and brought into play the additional factor of his mother's blood ties with Nezahualpilli. (See García Icazbalceta's introduction to the second volume of the <u>Nueva colección</u>, p. ix.)

LEXICAL DECOMPOSITION
OF COMPLEX VERB ROOTS IN SPANISH

CARL KIRSCHNER
Rutgers University

1. Introduction. The process of lexical decomposition, which helps the linguist arrive at a deep semantic structure (McCawley 1968b, Lakoff 1970) for a given complex verb root, is one which attempts to reduce these verbs to their most basic form, approximating the highest possible degree of abstraction. With his first case grammar model, Fillmore (1968) defined PROPOSITION as a predicator (verbal or adjectival) and one or more case roles, each associated with the verb in a specific case relationship. Cook (1973) established a case grammar model which can account for case roles which do not appear in the surface structure. These totally covert case roles may be lexicalized into the surface form of the verb. Consider structure (1).

(1) Juana soborna a María.   sobornar + [ABO*] / O lex.
    'Juana bribes María.'

The complex verb root <u>sobornar</u> 'bribe' lists three case roles, two of which have surfaced with the third, the Objective case, having been lexicalized into the surface form of the verb. The deep structure tree for (1) includes all three case roles.

(2)   S
        V   A   B   O
    Lexical prime   Juana   María   soborno

By extracting the lexicalized Objective case, the deep structure is left with a lexical prime, a predicate which carries a minimal semantic input. Lexical decomposition,

then, is the process in which totally covert case roles are
delexicalized from the complex verb root.

Using both generative semantic and case grammar theories
as a basis, this paper discusses the lexical decomposition
of complex verb roots in Spanish,[1] with special attention to
the poner types, so as to formulate some rules for their
generation from deep semantic structures. Complex verbs
account for a large percentage of Spanish predicates, and
many insights may be provided by their delexicalization.
Rules are hypothesized for both the delexicalization of
poner type complex verb roots and the generation of such
surface forms. Additionally, each lexical prime is shown
to have a specific semantic input, a fact which facilitates
the classification of predicates.

2. The hacer and dar type complex verb roots. Complex
verb roots of the hacer type may be divided into two groups:
those which are effective signal the creation of the Objective case while those which are affective signal an alteration or change in its nature. The effective hacer type
delexicalizations uncover a totally covert Objective case.
As a lexical prime, hacer carries the minimal semantic input
indicating 'creates' or 'composes'. Consider structure (3).

(3) Juana dibuja la casa.
'Juana draws the house.'

Structure (3) may be paraphrased as 'Juana creates a sketch
of the house', thereby indicating its effective nature. The
deep structure tree for (3) shows hacer as the lexical
prime.

(4)   S
    V   A   O
   hacer   Juana   dibujo

Whereas O has been lexicalized into the surface verb producing dibujar, it may also surface separately with the
lexical prime, yielding a synonymous structure and providing
a stylistic option for the speaker.[2]

(5) Juana hace un dibujo de la casa.
'Juana makes a sketch of the house.'

Although the effective hacer types delexicalize an Objective case role, the affective types show no delexicalized
case role. Rather, a stative adjective becomes a complex
verb root through the optional addition of a prefix, usually
en- or a-, and the obligatory addition of an infinitive
marker. The focus is not on any delexicalized case role

but rather on the stative adjective which comprises the complex verb root.

(6) Juana ensucia la blusa.
    'Juana dirties the blouse.'

The adjective sucio 'dirty' indicates that the Objective case has undergone a change. On a continuum which has as its two extremes sucio and limpio, ensuciar indicates a change toward the extreme representing sucio. The deep structure for the affective hacer types lists a predicate which is adjectival.

(7)   S
     V   A   O
     hacer sucio Juana   blusa

Although deep structure (4) allows for both a lexicalized and delexicalized surface structure form as in (3) and (5) respectively, structures like (7) do not, for there is no acceptable realization with hacer sucio. The affective hacer types appear to surface only in the lexicalized form. The deep structures for both the effective and affective hacer types, however, are two place predicates, with the arguments having an Agentive and an Objective function.

The dar type complex verb roots, however, are three place predicates. The arguments have Agentive, Benefactive, and Objective functions. Reconsidering sobornar in these terms, structure (2) requires the lexical prime dar which indicates 'change of possession'. As the Objective case soborno 'bribe' changes hands from the agent Juana to the benefactor María, sobornar may be classified as a dar type complex verb root. Consider structure (8) which represents the deep structure for sobornar using generative semantic terminology.

(8)   S
     P A_1 A_2 A_3
     dar   Juana   María   soborno

This structure is preferable in its versatility and economy for it facilitates the generating of two possible structures, structure (1) and its converse, in which Juana and María exchange roles as bribe giver and bribe receiver.

Whereas sobornar is a dar type which lexicalizes a tangible Objective case, many predicates, such as perdonar, lexicalize an intangible Objective case. Consider structure (9).

(9) El gobernador perdonó al criminal.
    'The governor pardoned the criminal.'

Structures such as (9) are generated from deep structures like that in (8). The delexicalized surface variations for (1) and (9) are indicated in (10) and (11) respectively.

(10) Juana le da el soborno a María.
   'Juana gives the bribe to María.'

(11) El gobernador le dió el perdón al criminal.
   'The governor gave the criminal the pardon.'

The <u>dar</u> type complex verb roots, then, are three place predicates formed by the lexicalization of the Objective case into the lexical prime <u>dar</u> which indicates change of possession. The effective <u>hacer</u> types are formed through similar lexicalization; however, they were shown to be two place predicates. The lexical prime <u>hacer</u> indicates either creation or alteration of the Objective case role.

3. The <u>poner</u> plus Objective type complex verb roots. Totally covert Objective cases have been uncovered in effective <u>hacer</u> type and <u>dar</u> type delexicalizations. Delexicalizations of the <u>poner</u> type will uncover either an Objective or a Locative case. Both <u>poner</u> types will have three deep structure arguments; they will function as Agentive, Objective, and Locative. In the case of the delexicalized Objective, the <u>poner</u> lexical prime indicates the placement of the specific Objective argument at, on, or in the specific Locative argument. Two such complex verb roots are <u>engrasar</u> 'grease' and <u>encolar</u> 'glue'.

(12) El mecánico engrasa la máquina.
   'The mechanic greases the machine.'

(13) El carpintero encola la mesa.
   'The carpenter glues the table.'

Structures (12) and (13) may be decomposed to (14) and (15) respectively, which are acceptable surface structures.

(14) El mecánico pone grasa en la máquina.
   'The mechanic puts grease in the machine.'

(15) El carpintero pone cola en la mesa.
   'The carpenter puts glue on the table.'

The delexicalized Objectives <u>grasa</u> 'grease' and <u>cola</u> 'glue' have been placed in the Locatives <u>máquina</u> 'machine' and <u>mesa</u> 'table' respectively. The deep structures have the lexical prime <u>poner</u> and three arguments.

(16)
```
            S
   P        A₁          A₂       A₃
 poner    mecánico     grasa    máquina
          carpintero   cola     mesa
```

The deep structure nodes for the lexical prime (P) and the delexicalized argument (A₂) represent the complex verb root. Arguments A₁ and A₃ may be varied to produce other engrasar and encolar surface structures as in (17) and (18).

(17) El hombre engrasa la rueda.
    'The man greases the wheel.'

(18) La niña encola la muñeca.
    'The child glues the doll.'

The poner plus delexicalized Objective type complex verb root seems to fit a specific pattern. Consider Figure 1.

Figure 1.

(a) poner / DELEX. O / en L
(b) en + LEX. O + r

Part (a) indicates that the poner and delexicalized Objective types are decomposed to poner which functions on the delexicalized Objective and positions it in, on, or at the Locative. Part (b) shows the formation of the complex root from the deep structure (en/GRASA/r → engrasar). Engrasar and encolar consist of a prefix, a lexicalized Objective, and an infinitive marker. Figure 1 apparently describes the functioning and formation of all poner + delexicalized Objective type complex verb roots.

4. The poner plus Locative type complex verb roots. The poner plus Locative type delexicalizations are similarly three place predicates. Consider structures (19) and (20) and their decomposed surface alternatives (21) and (22) respectively.

(19) El obrero ensaca el trigo.
    'The worker bags the wheat.'

(20) El detective encarcela al criminal.
    'The detective jails the criminal.'

(21) El obrero pone el trigo en sacos.
    'The worker puts the wheat in bags.'

(22) El detective pone el criminal en la carcel.
'The detective puts the criminal in jail.'

The deep structures for (19)-(22) are indicated in (23).

(23) S

P	A_1	A_2	A_3
poner	obrero	trigo	sacos
	detective	criminal	carcel

However, as the Objective case is put or placed at, on or in the delexicalized Locative, the complex verb root no longer has as constants P and A_2 in structure (23). Rather, P and A_3 represent the complex verb root with A_1 and A_2 varying according to the specific context. The formulas in Figure 2 explain the functioning and formation of ensacar 'bag' and encarcelar 'jail'.

Figure 2.

(a) poner /0/ en DELEX. L
(b) en + LEX. L + r

The formation of ensacar and encarcelar includes a prefix, a lexicalized Locative case, and an infinitive marker.

Although a prefix is present in many poner type complex verb roots, it is an optional factor as illustrated by cubrir 'cover'. Cubrir, however, presents a rather unusual situation.

(24) Juana cubre al niño.
'Juana covers the child.'

If cubrir is classified as a poner plus delexicalized Objective, then the delexicalized Objective cubierta 'cover' is put on the Locative niño 'child'. Cubrir then has a deep structure similar to (16) and is represented by Figure 1. If, however, the cover completely encompasses the child in the same way that infants are wrapped in blankets, then cubrir must be classified as a poner plus delexicalized Locative complex verb root. It will have a deep structure similar to (23) and will be represented by Figure 2. The Objective niño is put in the delexicalized Locative cubierta. Complex verb roots such as cubrir which require a double classification due to the versatility of the delexicalized case role are apparently limited in number.

5. Conclusion. The classification of complex verb roots according to their lexical primes receives support from their functioning within the framework of the generative semantic

36 / CARL KIRSCHNER

derivational mechanism. The causative paradigm for the poner type complex verb roots, which apparently is capable of generating all poner type complex verbs, lists three arguments and a preposition (PREP) at the stative level. Consider structure (25).

(25)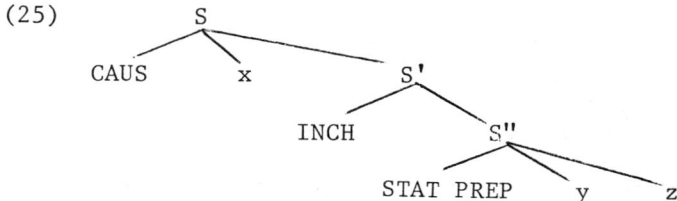

The presence of the PREP at the stative level is supported by Cook (1973:8) in his use of BE in, BE on, and BE at as the locative verbs for the stative level. Argument x assumes the Agentive function while y and z assume the Objective and Locative respectively. Insertion of lexical items into (25) produces (26).

(26)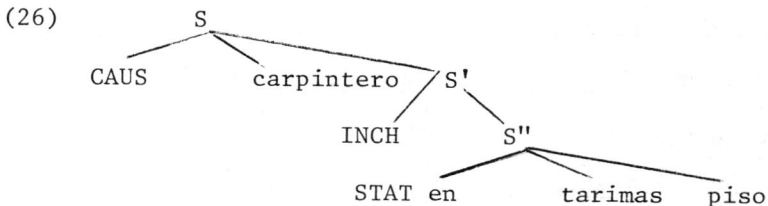

The permissible lexicalization of tarimas 'boards' (piso 'floor' may not be lexicalized) yields causative structure (27) while (28) results when the speaker opts for no lexicalization.

(27) El carpintero entarima el piso.
    'The carpenter floors the floor with boards.'

(28) El carpintero pone tarimas en el piso.
    'The carpenter puts boards on the floor.'

As the Objective tarimas is lexicalized into the surface form of the verb in (27), entarimar may be classified as a poner plus delexicalized Objective type complex verb root. Similarly, poner plus delexicalized Locative types may be generated from structure (25). In this case, however, Locative argument z rather than Objective argument y will be lexicalized. Structure (25) is apparently capable of functioning as the causative paradigm for all verbs classified under the lexical prime poner.

Complex verb roots have been classified as <u>hacer</u>, <u>dar</u>, or <u>poner</u> types. The <u>hacer</u> types were shown to be two place predicates, and their delexicalization uncovered an Objective case which underwent an effective change. With the affective <u>hacer</u> types, the focus was on the adjective which was incorporated into the predicate. The <u>dar</u> types were shown to be three place predicates, their delexicalization producing an Objective case and signaling a change in possession. The <u>poner</u> types were similarly three place predicates; however, their delexicalization uncovered either an Objective or a Locative case. Formulas were suggested to describe both the functioning and the formation of the <u>poner</u> types.

It has been shown for Spanish (Staczek 1976, Kirschner 1976) and for English (Cook 1971) that lexical primes are potential universals. The existence of a small number of lexical primes in Spanish would facilitate the classification and description of complex verb roots. Each lexical prime would have associated with it a causative paradigm capable of deriving the surface forms of the verb. Herein lies the apparent importance of lexical decomposition.

NOTES

1. Although they may be similarly decomposed and associated with a lexical prime, verbs of motion have been excluded from this discussion for they require special attention within the generative semantic derivational mechanism (causative paradigm).

2. Structure (5) and other decomposed surface realizations are, more accurately, potential synonomous forms. Their synonomy is dependent on presupposition, context, conveyed meaning and, to some degree, the specific lexical items filling the argument nodes. Whereas structures (13) and (15) are apparently synonomous indicating a purposeful 'gluing' by the 'carpenter', <u>encolar</u> 'glue' and <u>poner cola en</u> 'put glue on' may not be synonomous with the lexical items <u>niña</u> 'girl' and <u>muñeca</u> 'doll'. The complex verb root appears to signal a purposeful 'gluing' with these items, whereas the delexicalized structure (cf. (18)) seems to indicate accidental 'spreading or spilling of the glue'.

REFERENCES

Aid, Frances M. 1973. Semantic structures in Spanish: A proposal for instructional materials. Washington, D.C.: Georgetown University Press.

Anderson, John M. 1971. The grammar of case: Toward a localistic theory. Cambridge Studies in Linguistics, Number 4. Cambridge: Cambridge University Press.

Chafe, Wallace L. 1970. Meaning and the structure of language. Chicago: Chicago University Press.
Cook, Walter A., S.J. 1971. Improvements in case grammar. Georgetown University Papers on Languages and Linguistics, 2. 10-22. Washington, D.C.: Georgetown University Press.
Cook, Walter A., S.J. 1973. Covert case roles. Georgetown University Papers on Languages and Linguistics, 7. 52-81. Washington, D.C.: Georgetown University Press.
Cook, Walter A., S.J. 1974. Case grammar and generative semantics. Georgetown University Papers on Languages and Linguistics, 8. 1-28. Washington, D.C.: Georgetown University Press.
Kirschner, Carl. 1976. Generative semantics in Spanish. Unpublished Ph.D. dissertation, University of Massachusetts.
Kirschner, Carl. 1976. Localistic and nonlocalistic copulas in Spanish. Paper given at the 1976 LSA Summer Institute Colloquium on Hispanic and Luso-Brazilian Linguistics. Oswego: State University of New York at Oswego.
Lakoff, George. 1970. Irregularity in syntax. New York: Holt, Rinehart, and Winston.
McCawley, James D. 1968a. The role of semantics in a grammar. In: Universals in linguistic theory. Edited by Emmon Bach and Robert T. Harms. New York: Holt, Rinehart, and Winston. 124-169.
McCawley, James D. 1968b. Lexical insertion in a transformational grammar without deep structure. CLS 4.71-80. Chicago: Chicago University Press.
Staczek, John J. 1976. Decomposición léxica en español. Thesaurus, 31. Bogotá: Instituto Caro y Cuervo.

A LITERARY JARGON OF EARLY SPANISH DRAMA:
THE SAYAGUÉS DIALECT

JOHN LIHANI
University of Kentucky

There are at least as many varied approaches to the study of a dialectal lexicon as there are to the standard form of the language itself. From these many approaches, one can choose to make the type of study of the dialect he wants to: one can study the vocabulary, or morphology, phonology, or syntax of the language and can make the study as complete as one's time and desire permit him to do. My own approaches are presented in a recent book, <u>El lenguaje de Lucas Fernández: estudio del dialecto sayagués,</u>[1] in which I study and analyze the vocabulary, the phonology, the morphology, and the syntax of the Sayagués dialect, both synchronically, as it appeared in the work of Lucas Fernández and his contemporaries, and diachronically, as the speech developed to the sixteenth century from its foundation during the Vulgar Latin period.

My approaches, in brief, are broad, but conventional ones; and this paper will only sketch some of them, the methodology used, and some of the results drawn from the problems entailed in the study of a dialect which is based on literary sources.

The Sayagués jargon is found mostly in the language of Lucas Fernández. Fernández was a Spanish dramatist from Salamanca of the late fifteenth and early sixteenth centuries (1474-1542). His plays are replete with pastoral dialogues expressed in a colloquial form of the Leonese dialect, nowadays called by the conventional literary name of Sayagués. The above-named study of the dialect is divided into two parts (1) a linguistic analysis, and (2) a lexicon.

The name for the dialect itself has a peculiar semantic history. Etymologically, Sayagués refers to the dialect of

Sayago, an agricultural town which is located in the southwest portion of the province of Zamora, Western Spain. But the term, Sayagués, was very early misapplied to designate the rustic speech of the region of Salamanca, even though the dialect of Salamanca, strictly speaking, should be labeled Charro or Charruno, and certainly not Sayagués.

Thus, in the theater of the early Spanish dramatists, such as Lucas Fernández and Juan del Encina, both of whom grew up in Salamanca, we find what is a representation of the Salamancan dialect called Charro. Therefore, the literary critics who began to call Encina's and Fernández's dialect 'Sayagués', after the town of Sayago, were actually using a misnomer for the Charro dialect of Salamanca. Dramatists like Bartolomé de Torres Naharro, Gil Vicente, Lope de Rueda, and even Lope de Vega and Tirso de Molina imitated the dialect of Encina and Fernández and spiced the speech of their rustics with the jargon; but it was Lucas Fernández, a native of Salamanca, who used the dialect with the greatest degree of authenticity. It is for this reason, the fact that Lucas Fernández was the most authentic user of the Sayagués dialect, that his language has been the focus of Sayagués studies.

Although the dialect was in existence for many centuries prior to the Renaissance period, the term Sayagués was first applied to the dialect of the Spanish rustics, only around the middle of the sixteenth century. In 1567 Juan de Timoneda published Lope de Rueda's plays and wrote that Lope de Rueda was an 'espejo y guía de ... sayagos y estilo cabañero'. But Lope de Rueda based his dialect, not on the real Sayagués, but rather on the racy dialect of Encina and Lucas Fernández, both of whom, as we have noted, used the Charro dialect of Salamanca in their plays. So the confusion of Sayagués with Charro is clearly manifest by the middle of the sixteenth century.

By the beginning of the seventeenth century, the term Sayagués became synonymous with the term 'barbarous', and with this new adjectival meaning, Sayagués is seen registered in Sebastián de Covarrubias' dictionary of 1611.[2] There are other indications which show that Sayagués came to be applied not only to Sayago and its people, but by extension, Sayagués came to have a figurative meaning of tonto, bárbaro, and rústico.

Miguel de Cervantes in 1615 contrasts the coarse speech of Sayago, on the one hand, with the cultured speech of Toledo, on the other. The speech of Sayago, to Miguel de Cervantes, represented the general, nonstandard dialects of Spanish, while the speech of Toledo, represented the standard, normal Castilian. In Cervantes' novel, Don Quijote de la Mancha (1615), Don Quijote reprimands his squire, Sancho Panza, for having said friscal instead of fiscal, and calls him 'prevaricador del buen lenguaje', while Sancho defends himself by saying that he was not educated in the city, and so an uncouth 'Sayagues', like himself, should not be expected to talk like a city-slicker from Toledo.[3]

In fact, during the Golden Age of Spanish letters, the term Sayagués became conventionally used to refer to uncultured individuals. And today, the misnomer, Sayagués, is so frequently used in Spanish literary criticism, that we have come to accept it, against our better judgment, as a valid term, for any nonstandard, dialectal variety of Spanish. Basically, the dialect is the same as the standard language both in vocabulary and syntax. The dialect does differ from the accepted language in some lexical items, in morphology; but especially, its differences are phonological.

The dialect, since it is a nonstandard speech, is not restricted by normative rules, as is generally true of the standard language. Therefore, greater freedom of usage is bound to exist in the dialect than does in the standard language. Inconsistencies within the same dialect can, therefore, occur more frequently than they do in the standard language, because there is no sweeping normative rule to abrogate them from the language or, on the other hand, to normalize them. Inconsistencies in a dialect are found in any facet of the speech, and so will occur in pronunciation, in the lexicon, to a lesser degree in morphology, and even in syntax.

The dialectal inconsistencies and deviations from the standard language produced comic situations that the Spanish Renaissance dramatists were quick to take advantage of. The dialect, as an off-standard speech, was used to convey and achieve comic effect. But along with humor, the dialect also served as a vehicle for translating people's feelings of discontent into words of social criticism. Even in the medieval period, the jester was the unique commoner who could dare to criticize the emperor and be able to get away with it. So in the turbulent Renaissance, the Spanish dramatists often took the role of the medieval jester, and would profit by the freedom accorded to them by the free and open nature of the dialect. Lucas Fernández and Torres Naharro, for example, would dare to criticize, with relative impunity, the very princes and lords of the Church who came to see and enjoy their plays.[4] They would remind their particular audiences during the difficult economic period of the sixteenth century, 'Vos, señores, ... coméis de los sudores de pobres manos ajenas', and they would censure the highest authority by proclaiming that the pope 'se está en Roma con sus vicios'. Thus, along with the structural approaches to the lexicon of a dialect, there also intermingle the sociolinguistic as well as the psycholinguistic approaches.

The lexical approach reveals some of the archaic characteristics of the Sayagués. Being a dialect, Sayagués retains more archaic expressions than does the standard Castilian language. This is generally true of dialects: they tend to be more conservative than is their counterpart of the standard language. Hence, we find archaic terms as <u>cholla</u> for <u>cabeza</u>, <u>aínas</u> for <u>pronto</u>, <u>asina</u> for <u>así</u>, and <u>aqueste</u> for <u>este</u>.

Then there are those vocabulary terms that are peculiarly dialectal: <u>aosadas</u> 'certainly', <u>soncas</u> 'truly', <u>carillo</u> 'brother', <u>chapado</u> ' pretty', <u>quillotro</u> 'whatchamacallit', <u>asmar</u> 'think', <u>ñembrar</u> 'remember', and exclamations such as <u>pardiez</u> 'by Gads', <u>ñoramala</u> 'bad hour', and <u>juria San Pabro</u> 'I swear to St. Paul'. These are typical dialectal expressions of Sayagués.

From a phonological approach, the shepherd dialect used by the early Spanish dramatists, also holds some evident peculiarities. The Sayagués dialect in Juan del Encina, Lucas Fernández, Bartolomé de Torres Naharro, and Gil Vicente[5] normally palatalizes the initial nasal and lateral sounds. Thus, a shepherd from a play by Lucas Fernández is bound to say <u>ño</u> for <u>no</u> or <u>ñunca</u> for <u>nunca</u> and <u>llugar</u> for <u>lugar</u>.

The change of a consonant into <u>r</u>, or rhotacism, is another phonological characteristic of Sayagués. It is usually the <u>l</u>, preceded by an occlusive (sometimes by a fricative) that produces the <u>r</u>. And so we have <u>púbrico</u> for <u>público</u>, <u>pracer</u> instead of <u>placer</u>, <u>concrusión</u> for <u>conclusión</u>, <u>fraqueza</u> for <u>flaqueza</u>, and <u>obrigado</u> for <u>obligado</u>. The similarity to Portuguese is quite manifest in some of these terms. But vacillation of the <u>r</u> and <u>l</u> is quite widespread, and can remind us also of non-Indo-European languages like Chinese and Japanese. Presumably, the older the language, the more confused the two liquids <u>l</u> and <u>r</u> become.

As we have noted, a dialect is not bound by strict grammatical rules, as is more likely the case with the standard language. If a change goes in one direction in a dialect, it can turn around and go in the opposite direction. For example, if Castilian <u>obligado</u> comes out in Sayagués as <u>obrigado</u>, then <u>temprano</u>, through hypercorrection, becomes <u>templano</u>. Similarly, <u>prado</u> through hypercorrection, becomes <u>plado</u>. This lambdacism is found particularly in the works of Gil Vicente, possibly because he was Portuguese, and his knowledge of the Spanish jargon may have been tinged with a bit of uncertainty and impreciseness.

Among other consonantal deviations from the standard language, we find the dialectal aspiration of the <u>h</u>, which is silent in Castilian, and we also find the change of <u>f</u> to <u>h</u>. This aspiration is an archaic feature which is retained in dialect form. And so in Sayagués, we hear <u>habrar</u> for

Castilian, (h)ablar, hermoso for (h)ermoso, huego for fuego, and huerte for fuerte. The Spanish lexicographer, Covarrubias, living in Toledo in 1611, still pronounced the h in some of these words, and those people who did not pronounce the aspiration, he claimed were 'pusilánimes, descuidados, y de pecho flaco'.

Besides the differences in consonants that stand out clearly in the Sayagués jargon, there are likewise differences from Castilian in the quality of the vowels. Vacillations arise between o and u and i and e. And thus among many examples we find that matrimonio becomes matrimuño, muchacha becomes mochacha, and decir becomes dicir.

Some vowels, on the other hand, diphthongize in the Sayagués when they do not do so in Castilian. For example, Sayagués has apriende for Castilian aprende, sueldado for soldado and prepuésito for propósito. The dialect will also show some metatheses, like majestad which becomes jamestad, and Salamanca that turns into Masalanca in the dialect.

Among the linguistic aspects and lexical elements already mentioned here, the diachronic approach to phonology results in recognition of patterns such as that of the sound shift of initial Latin f- to h- to zero (∅), or the palatal voiced sibilant [ž] changing to the unvoiced dorsoalveolar, or the apicoalveolar, sibilant [s], particularly as this shift is seen in the change of the indirect object pronoun ge to se. This happens when the indirect object pronoun is followed by another pronoun beginning with a lateral fricative, as is seen in the development of the Latin illi illum passing through ge lo [že lo] to se lo.

From the morphological approach, the variations in the dialectal usage emphasize the inconsistencies like those that happen in the verbal endings, -aron, -oron, -istes, -istéis, and for the second person singular pronouns vos-tú: sabés, sabéis, sabes, etc.

In the study of the dialectal lexicon, the semantic approach points out the need for a redefinition of certain terms. Terms like carillo 'beloved-brother, friend' and tempero 'cold wind, soil moisture' are discovered with a preference for the second meanings in the dialect. And, of course, the etymological approach bears testimony to the fact that many difficulties still remain, and even abound, in the Sayagués as they do in the Spanish lexicon.

In sum, a composite use of various approaches to the study of a dialect which is based principally on written sources of a literary nature, proves to be of considerable interest. It is apparent that in this complex world, and in the complexity of languages, there is much room for the time-tested, traditional approaches to the study of a dialectal lexicon, as there is also room for, and indeed the need for, the novel and the unusual approaches to the fascinating subject of language.

NOTES

1. J. Lihani, <u>El lenguaje de Lucas Fernández: estudio del dialecto sayagués</u> (Bogotá: Instituto Caro y Cuervo, 1973).
2. Sebastián de Covarrubias y Orozco, <u>Tesoro de la lengua castellana o española</u>, ed. Martín de Riquer (Barcelona: S. A. Horta, 1943).
3. Miguel de Cervantes Saavedra, <u>Don Quijote de la Mancha</u>, ed. F. Rodríguez Marín (Madrid: Espasa Calpe, 1944), Part II, Ch. 19, p. 19.
4. Lucas Fernández, <u>Farsas y églogas</u>, ed. J. Lihani (New York: Las Americas, 1969); Bartolomé de Torres Naharro, <u>Propalladia</u>, ed. J. E. Gillet, Vol. 2 (Bryn Mawr: University of Pennsylvania Press, 1946).
5. Juan del Encina, <u>Eglogas</u>, ed. H. López Morales (Madrid: Escelicer, 1963); Lucas Fernández, <u>Farsas y églogas</u>; Bartolomé de Torres Naharro, <u>Propalladia</u>; Gil Vicente, <u>Obras dramáticas castellanas</u>, ed. T. R. Hart (Madrid: Espasa Calpe, 1962).

LEXICAL CORRESPONDENCES BETWEEN METROPOLITAN AND CANADIAN FRENCH

RALEIGH MORGAN, JR.
University of Michigan

This study in structural dialectology will be concerned with the phonemic system of a variety of Quebec French as compared with varieties of Metropolitan speech. The Quebec data were collected by the writer, over a period of four years starting in 1967, in County Beauce, located in the Chaudière River Valley, south of Quebec City. My informants were direct descendants of the first settlers, who came to Beauce in 1736 under the French seigneurial system.

It has been demonstrated by Moulton (1960) why a listing of phonemes and their patterning is inadequate for comparing closely related dialects. One must include lexical correspondences in such a study. To do only an inventory is likely to show that the dialects under study have an identical set of phonemes, yet everyone is keenly aware that the dialects are 'different'. This 'difference' results from the fact that the incidence of phonemes is not the same. This study, both structural and historical, will give attention to the geographic distribution of features. Emphasis will be on stressed vowels in open and closed syllables in vocabulary items, common to three varieties of French: Paris, Burgundy, and County Beauce, Quebec. Paris was chosen because of the role of its speech as a norm in the Francophone world. Burgundy has certain features, which characterize the periphery, north of Paris. This fact has relevance in view of the provenance of the first settler of New France. In addition, there will be a discussion of features shared by varieties of French and French based Creoles throughout this hemisphere.

In his study of contemporary French pronunciation, Martinet (1971:209) presents the following vowel phoneme inventory for stressed vowels in the Paris region:[1]

Figure 1. Phonemes of the Paris region.

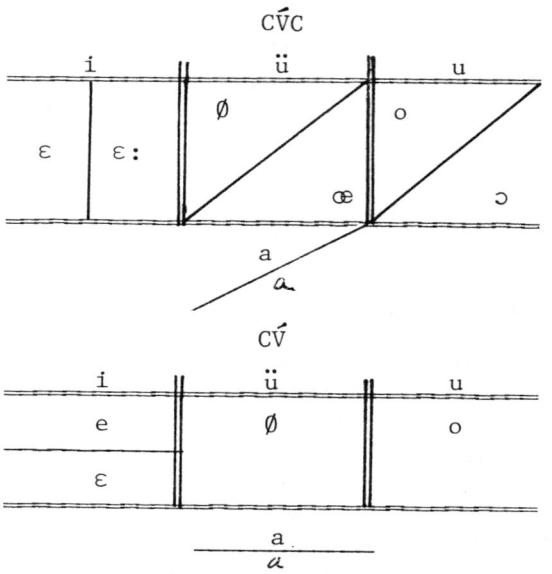

It will be noted that, in open syllables, there are quality contrasts between the mid-front and low vowels. In Paris, quality contrasts are neutralized in the case of /ø/ and /o/ in open syllables. On the other hand, there are contrasts between all mid and low vowels in closed syllables. In this type of syllable, high percentages were tabulated for the Martinet informants, who distinguished between belle and bêle on the basis of a quantity difference alone and between patte-pâte, sotte-saute, jeune-jeûne by a combination of both quality and quantity. The Martinet informants were army officers born between 1910 and 1921. A sequel to this study was done by Ruth Reichstein (1960). Miss Reichstein's informants were Paris school girls, born between 1940 and 1945, and, in her research, she sought to ascertain the degree to which certain contrasts were maintained among various social classes in attendance at different types of schools in several kinds of communities. Starting with some of the same oppositions used in the Martinet study, Reichstein's results showed an increasing loss of phonological oppositions, such as belle-bêle, patte-pâte. Loss of these contrasts could be correlated with school type, social class, and community.

For Burgundy, Martinet (1971:211) catalogued quantity contrasts for high, mid, and low vowels regardless of syllable structure. An especially interesting finding was the existence in open syllables of three contrasting mid-front vowels.[2] Galand (1968) brings our view of the Burgundy system into even greater focus with his paper on vowel oppositions in a variety of Burgundian French, spoken in the Dheune region of Southeast France. Here high vowels have quantity contrasts in all syllable types. In the case of low vowels, the opposition is mainly between anterior and posterior a, although some speakers may have quantity as the only distinctive feature. For mid-back vowels, quality is the dominant feature in both syllable types, i.e. /ɔ/ versus /o/ in sotte-saute, sot-saut. For this latter pair there is the new trend of displacing /ɔ/ in open syllables by /o/. Contrast is then maintained by quantity, e.g. /so/ 'sot' versus /so:/ 'saut'. The pair jeune 'young' and jeûne 'fast' are kept distinct primarily by distinctive quality, although, in all syllable types, the tense phone of the pair is accompanied by length, i.e. /zœ̃n/ and /z̃ø:n/. In the mid-front series we find /ɛ/ in contrast with /e/ and /e:/. This three-way opposition maintains not only lexical contrasts, but grammatical ones as well, e.g. piquait (imperfect), piqué (past participle) and piquez (2 plural).

The phonemic inventory is as follows:

Figure 2. Phonemes of Burgundy.

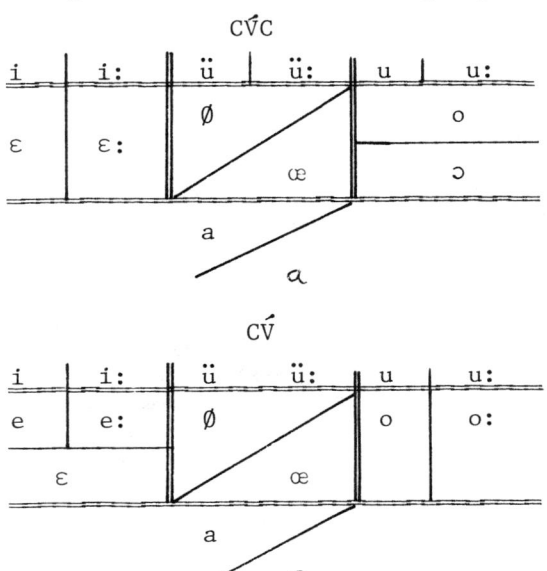

In the French of County Beauce, several phenomena merit our attention. In closed syllables, high vowels occur as lax allophones, e.g. dit beside dix [dᶻIs], du and dur [dUr], bout beside bouche [bŬs].³ Mid and low vowels have quality distinctions, but we find also minimal pairs, in which both quality and quantity are distinctive features.

It must be said that quality is the feature which transcends the whole system and quantity must be regarded as redundant. Noteworthy is the fact that this length is actualized as diphthongization, e.g. [mei̯t] 'maître' and [mɛt] 'mettre', [zø̯yn] 'jeûne' and [zœn] 'jeune', [pa̯ut] 'pâte' and [pat] 'patte'. Cases of phonotactic length will occur also as diphthongization. In view of the history of phonologically relevant length in the lexemes involved, this writer has chosen to analyze diphthongization in such cases as phonemic length. In open syllables, there are contrasts based on quality distinctions for both mid-front and back vowels. In this environment, however, low vowels are completely absent. The reason will soon be clear. The system for Quebec may be represented as follows:

Figure 3. Phonemes of County Beauce, Quebec.

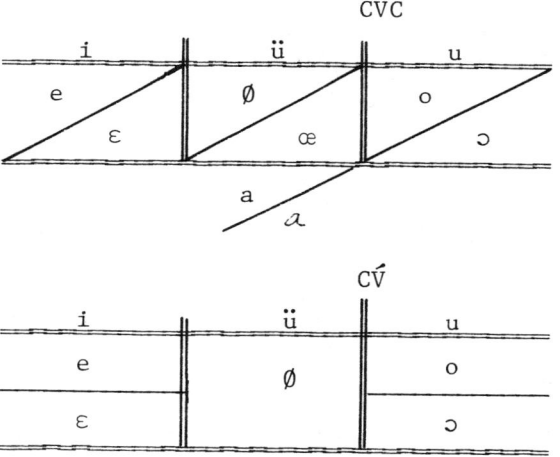

Inspection of the inventories for Paris, Burgundy, and Beauce permits several generalizations. Burgundy is, of course, unique with its distinctive quantity for all high vowels as well as three e-phonemes. Unlike Quebec, both Paris and Burgundy use quantity alone to distinguish belle and bêle (cf. use of both quantity and quality for maître and mettre in Quebec). Burgundy uses quantity as the sole distinct feature to separate piqué and piquez, sot and saut. Quality and quantity are used by all three to distinguish jeune from jeûne, patte from pâte. This is also the case for cote and côte in Paris and Beauce, unlike the use of quality only for saute-sotte in Burgundy. It will be noted that quantity is never a distinctive feature in open syllables in either Paris or Quebec. In Beauce all mid vowels in closed syllables may combine timbre and length to distinguish minimal pairs. This is also true in France for

Normandy, the Eastern sector, and the Southwest (Martinet 1971:214).4

We find a new distribution pattern in both Burgundy and Beauce. In Paris, the mid-back vowels contrast only in closed syllables and are in complementary distribution in open ones. Galand (1968:170) presents the contrast between /ɔ/ and /o:/ in open syllables as the norm for Burgundy and states that such contrasts are very characteristic of toponyms, regional terms, as well as of the common vocabulary. This pronunciation is menaced, however, by the spread of a purely quantitative opposition between /o/ and /o:/. The /o/ and /ɔ/ contrast seems stable in County Beauce.

Thus far we have discussed how the three varieties differ in distribution patterns and how they exploit quantity and quality in the economy of the language. Distribution and distinctive features give a view of structural relations on the synchronic level. The history of the language is reflected in the incidence of phonemes in the shared lexical stock. Additional data may also be extracted from French based Creoles for this reason.

Prior to an analysis of lexical correspondences in the several varieties of French, a statement should be made about the origins of French vowel systems. Proto-Italo-West Romance (hereinafter PIW) had a phonemic system in which vowel quality and consonantal quantity were distinctive features. Vowels developed nondistinctive quantity in open syllables. When intervocalic geminate consonants simplified in Gallo-Romance, vowel quantity then became phonologically distinct, e.g. pĕnna 'feather' and pēna (<poena) 'penalty' > pĕna, pēna respectively (Haudricourt and Juilland 1970:45f.). Proto-French thus doubled its inventory. From this point on, the Francien treatment of long vowels, as opposed to the short, diverged from most of the other Romance languages. The diphthong au was incorporated into the long vowel series and led eventually to the diphthongization of long ā. Both ultimately simplified to ǭ and ę̄, reducing the phonetic interval between phonemes of the mid-front and back series. Haudricourt and Juilland (1970:55f.) see this event as the reason for the subsequent diphthongization of older ẹ̄ and ǭ and eventually that of ē and ō. Later Francien developments include the fronting of PIW /u/ to /ü/ and the shift of the diphthongs u̯o < ǭ and ou̯ < ō to the mid-front rounded vowels.5

Comparison of high vowels in our charts shows that lexical correspondences match in all varieties, even if one takes into account the allophones of Beauce and the quantity of Burgundy. In terms of etymological source, however, French /u/ is not the direct descendant of PIW /u/. The sources of French /u/ are primarily short ǒ (gout < gǒta < gǔtta) and long ǭ (joug < iǭgu < iǔgu). Additional sources are due to the coalescence and subsequent development of diphthongs such as a + u (clou < clāvu), au + u (trou < traucu), ǫ̆ + u (fous < fǫlles) (Rheinfelder 1953).

All varieties have anterior and posterior a, although neither phoneme occurs in open syllables in Beauce. These two vowels represent a French innovation. Proto-Gallo-Romance short ă is the source of these low vowels, e.g. chat < căttu, bas < băssu, battre *băttĕre < battuĕre, partir < părtire, and others. The phoneme /a/ became velarized in certain environments in French. One such environment was before /-rr-/. There is evidence that the opposition of intervocalic single r and geminate r was retained relatively late in French. Martinet (1949:38) believes that geminate r was often articulated as a velar or laryngeal phoneme as opposed to the apical articulation of simple r and it was thus before laryngeal r that a velarized.[6] Velarization also took place in other situations, e.g. in connection with vowel lengthening, due to the contraction of vowels in hiatus (Old French eage < âge), or, due to the loss of a following consonant (Old French paste < pâte) (cf. Pope 1952:212).

The most striking event in the history of anterior and posterior a in Quebec is the merger of these two vowels with /ɔ/ in open syllables and when accented. This has resulted in a major change in lexical correspondences between Metropolitan and Canadian French. Affected are Beauce reflexes of words such as bas, chat, pas. In such words the archiphoneme /A/ must have velarized in successive stages to a very low and posterior articulation, thus overlapping the phonetic interval between posterior a and /ɔ/ (Moulton 1960: 178). A merger must have been facilitated by the zero functional load between the two low vowels and /ɔ/ in open syllables prior to the merger. We know already, from contemporary sources, that there was no quality contrast between mid-back vowels about 1700 (Martinet 1946) and, even now, such a contrast is rare or unstable in the Francophone world (Martinet 1971:205-217).

In addition to the merger in open syllables, the archiphoneme /A/ merges with /ɔ/ before s and r, e.g. /ipɔs/ 'il passe' or /ipɔr/ 'il part'. Gendron (1966:90f.) compares what he calls 'a postérieure sombre' in il part with the phoneme /ɔ/ and concludes that the two vowels (e.g. in part and port) have a very similar articulation, have no 'différences auditives sensibles' and that the two vowels are really 'à peu de chose près identiques'. My auditory impression confirms the Gendron statement and so we phonemicize /bɔ/ 'bas', /šɔ/ 'chat', /pɔs/ 'passe', /pɔr/ 'part' in those words, which originally had the archiphoneme /A/, rather than use the symbols [ɒ] or [å].

The above lexemes, in which the low vowels have merged with /ɔ/, should be compared with lexemes containing the sequence spelled oi. In the chart of correspondences (see Chart 1), we see mois 'month' and bois 'woods' listed under /ɔ/ with bas, chat, passe, part. The pronoun moi is under /e/. Paris moi and mois contrast with Beauce /mwe/ (pronoun) and /mwɔ/ 'month'. The history of oi will reveal why this is so. By using English loanwords or Canadian lexemes as examples, one can trace the diphthongal stages through which older Proto-Gallo-Romance long ē passed and establish the chronology of the event. There was not just a unilateral development of this vowel, but, at its various stages, it coalesced with identical diphthongs from other sources. Eventually all end as /wA/ in modern standard French, i.e. stages represented by English veil, Leroy, choice, voice or Quebec /mwe/ are now equivalent to Paris voile, (le) roi, choix, voix, and moi. (See Chart 2 and Shorter Oxford English Dictionary s.v.v. veil, royal, choice, voice.)

Chronologically the 'veil' stage represents the second diphthongization affecting the long tense mid vowels in Proto-French, dating from the sixth century. The 'Leroy' or 'choice' stage dates from the twelfth century and the

Chart 1. Lexical Correspondences.

Vowel	Quebec	Paris	Burgundy
u	loup, debout	loup, goutte	loup, goutte
U	goutte, dbUt		
u:			loue, goûte
ü	bu	bu, (il)cuve	bu, (il)cuve
Ü	(il)cuve		
ü:			due, (la)cuve
i	ami	ami, (qu'il) rive	ami, (qu'il) rive
I	(qu'il) rive		
i:			amie, (la)rive
a	patte, partent /harb/	bat, patte, moi	bat, patte, moi
ɑ	pâte	bas, pâte, mois	bas, pâte, mois
o	saut, chose, côte	saut, chose, côte	saut, chose, côte
ɔ	bas, chat, part, port, mois	cotte, port	sot, cotte, port
ø	jeu, jeûne	jeu, jeûne	jeu, jeûne
œ	jeune, une	jeune	jeune
e	-é, moi, maître	-é	-é
e:			-ez
ɛ	-ait, mettre, adr t	-ait, maître, mettre	-ait

Chart 2. Evolution of Proto-French ẹ̄.

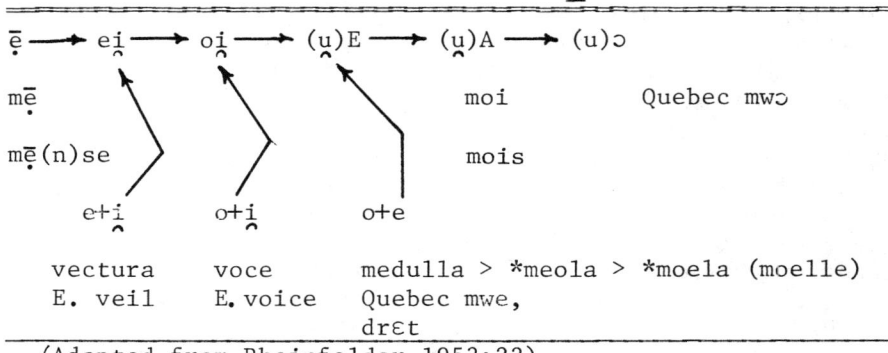

(Adapted from Rheinfelder 1953:22)

'mwe' stage of Quebec the thirteenth (LaChaussee 1974:189, 197, 201; Rheinfelder 1953:I, 22; Brunot et Bruneau 1949: 80). From the fourteenth century, we learn that /we/ is affected by several tendencies. Dauzat (1928) speaks of the growing cleavage between lexemes caused by the tendency to reduce /wɛ/ to /ɛ/, e.g. the pronunciation /frwɛt/ 'froid' alternating with /frɛt/, /krwɛ/ 'craie' alternating with /krɛr/ or /krwar/, /mwe/ 'moi' with /mwa/, /frãswe/, now François, in alternation with what is present français. These few examples give some clue to the final result. In fact each word has its own history. We know that /frwɛt/ displaced /frɛt/ to ultimately become modern standard froid, but /krɛ/ for 'chalk' became standard instead of /krwɛ/. At one point in time /krwɛr/ was favored over /krɛr/ as the norm for 'believe', but both were ultimately relegated to 'patois' status by croire. The pronoun /mwe/ 'moi' remained the norm for some five hundred years and, during the ancien régime, it became identified with court speech. In post-revolutionary France, this court norm was displaced by /mwa/, a popular innovation in existence since the fourteenth century. The language has maintained both François (Beauce frãswe) and français, but the former has become lexicalized as a proper name (see Chart 3).

What is very clear from the Beauce data is that this development had not run its full course, when the language was transplanted to New France in the seventeenth century. As seen in the examples, /we/, /e/ and /wA/ gave different results in different words. In some words the /wA/ pronunciation established itself prior to the post-revolutionary period. Beauce shows this early cleavage in the opposition of /mwe/ 'moi', /žbwe/ 'je bois', /frãswe/ 'François'; /frɛt/ 'froid', /adrɛt/ 'adroit', français in opposition to /mwɔ/ 'mois', /bwɔ/ '(le)bois', /trwɔ/ 'trois', and others.[7] In fact, this pattern /wE/ and /E/ in contrast with /wɔ/ or /wA/

Chart 3. Evolution of oi.

Word	End XII	XIII	XIV	XVI	XVII	XVIII	XIX
moi	moi̯	mwe	mwe* / mwa	mwe* / mwa	mwe* / mwa	mwe° / mwa*	mwe / mwa*
craie	kroi̯	krwe	krwe-kre	kre*	kre*	kre*	kre*
croi	kroi̯rə	krwerə	kwerə* / krwarə / krerə	krwerə* / krwarə / krerə°	krwerə* / krwarə / krer*	krwer° / krwar* / krer	krwar* / krwer
-ait	etoi̯t	etwe	etwe	etwe* / ete°	ete* / etwe°	ete*	ete*

Legend: * = norm; ° = formal, court, pedantic
(Adapted from Brunot et Bruneau:80)

can be regarded as typical of other varieties of French and French based Creoles of this hemisphere from Northern North America to the Antilles. It is true, of course, that the same structural pattern may be realized by 'geographic allophones' (Moulton 1960:177). In Acadian, we have /awɛr/ 'avoir' and /harnwɑ/ 'harnais'; in Missouri, /wɛr/ 'voir' and /bwa/ '(le)bois'; in Haitian Creole, /dwe/ 'devoir' (verb) and /devwɑ/ 'devoir' (noun); and in Martiniquan Creole /zetwɛl/ 'etoile' and /zwɑ/ '(l')oie'.[8]

It must be noted, however, that there are some areas where this structural pattern is not found. The Hull data for Windsor, Ontario show /mwa/ 'pronoun' versus /mwa/ 'mois', i.e. anterior versus posterior a. One finds, nevertheless, forms such as /frɛt/ and /drɛt/ in Windsor. Hull (1955:36) suggests the hypothesis that Windsor formerly had /mwɛ/ and /frɛt/ in opposition to /mwå/, but the opening of /mwɛ/ to /mwa/ is part of a wider change of final /ɛ/ to /a/, e.g. il fait became /ifa/ in this dialect. This phenomenon is a Windsor innovation, thus driving a wedge between Quebec, the Maritimes, and Missouri. Louisiana has /frɛt/ as elsewhere, but /bwa/ 'boire' versus /bwɑ/ '(le)bois' (Morgan 1959). In their data for Lafayette, Conwell and Juilland (1963) show only /wa/ in these words. Ditchy (1932) published an anonymous manuscript, dating from the turn of the century, which records the language, history, and folklore of the last descendants of the Acadians, who established themselves in Louisiana in the eighteenth century. In the Glossaire of this manuscript, we find entries such as aweine 'avoine', boëte 'boîte', vouèr, 'voir', drètement 'précisément' as opposed to droit, adroit, assoir.[9] This Acadian document seems to indicate that the language described has the same structure as Quebec and the Maritimes. How does one explain the different structure in data collected in more recent years? Studies of non-English speech in Louisiana prior to 1940 mention the existence of Colonial French,

Acadian and Creole (Lane 1934). Guilbeau (1972:47) uses the term General Louisiana French, the result of leveling of all three types of speech due to absorption and mutual influence (cf. Morgan 1970). The /wA/ sequence in more recent Louisiana data may be the consequence of the spread of certain features of standard Colonial throughout the state. It should be remembered that settlers from France imported the language into Lower Louisiana about a century later than in New France or in the Antilles.

As we complete our analysis of lexical correspondences, one sees little difference between the three varieties in the pronunciation of words like saut, chose, côte (from săltu, causa, cŏsta respectively). In Beauce, côte has a long vowel actualized as a diphthong. In Louisiana, /o/ opens to /ɔ/ in words like chose. In the case of jeune and jeûne (from iŏvene and ieunat < ieiunāre respectively), all varieties show uniform correspondences on the structural level, although the opening of /ü/ in une to /œ/ or the shift of /e/ in chez to /ø/ are typical of speech of Beauce. If the merger of /ɛ̃/ and /œ̃/ in Metropolitan French may be explained as due to low functional load (Martinet 1972:147f.), we may offer the opening of the vowel in the feminine indefinite article as an additional reason for shifting the vowel of the masculine article to the /ɛ̃/ column. Mention has already been made of the fact that the sequence /we/ has raised the frequency of occurrence of the /e/. The main sources of this vowel are words derived from etyma with Latin accented long ā in open syllables, e.g. nez < nāsu, pré < prātu, -er < -āre, -é < -ātu, -ez < -atis. The developmental stages might be represented as ā > aȇ > ȇ > ē. The phoneme /ɛ/ is from a variety of sources, but primarily from e: perd < pĕrdit and fève < fāba, Mai < Māiu. The vowel from pĕrdit was later joined by ā in the latter lexemes in an evolutionary sequence similar to that indicated for /e/.

This discussion could treat other phenomena, which characterize Quebec French. A full description of vowels would include vowel desonorization and syncope, both affecting syllable structure. As for consonants, one must mention the affrication of dental stops and the neutralization of velar and palatal contrasts. Affrication remains a purely phonetic phenomenon, but the neutralization of the velar-palatal opposition achieves greater economy of distinctive features. This is partially illustrated by the use of the velar nasal in Beauce for /ñ/, e.g. ligne [liŋ]. Structurally this /ŋ/ makes the velar order, now /k-g-ŋ/, parallel to /p-b-m/ and /t-d-n/. Within each order each phone is distinct by one pertinent feature (sonority or nasality). Horizontally, each series is parallel with one distinct feature distinguishing each (point of articulation) (Martinet 1955:68f.). Although affrication is a phonetic phenomenon in Quebec French, analogous cases of assimilation have had an interesting result outside Quebec. In Acadian, velar stops before front vowels merge with dental stops, e.g.: queue /tjɛ/, gueule /djɛl/. In Louisiana, velars and dentals in such environments merge together as /c̃j̃/. In Missouri, on the other hand, dental stops before /j/ merge with velar stops, e.g. métier /mekje/ and diable /gjɑb/.

In this study my analysis of the common vocabulary has shown few etymological differences, but several principles may be highlighted. The following points should be considered:

(1) An etymological difference may be the result of fluctuations in usage at an earlier period. The alternation of /wɛ/ and /ɛ/ has already been discussed. The fluctuation of /ɛ/ and /a/ before /r/ is recorded throughout the New World and loan words in English document this, e.g. merchant-marchand, sargeant-sergent, clerk, Clark-clerc. In Quebec and throughout the hemisphere we find /šaršə/ for chercher, /harb/ for gerbe, /parmi/ for permis, /parsɔn/ for personne, and others.

(2) The variety of French may reflect an earlier stage in the phonological history of the language. The history of the oi sequence is highlighted by the Quebec evidence. We learn also from these data that there was, in addition, fluctuation between /wA/ and /A/, i.e.: /krwɔ/ '(la)croix' and /lakradtãperãs/ 'la croix de temperance' in contrast with /krwɛr/ 'croire' and /žkre/ 'je crois'.

(3) Types of phonemic change are brought into relief. The development of an anterior and posterior a is the example of a split occurring in French probably as early as the sixteenth century. We find relexes of this split in all varieties, although recent research shows this to be an unstable opposition (Martinet 1971, Reichstein 1960). Our comparison of lexical correspondences shows that, in this case, Quebec has gone a step further and added a merger along with the split (A → ɔ) in port-part/partent, chat/chatte). This split with merger is used to maintain lexical contrasts, such as moi/mois, and the like. This is a device that Paris has lost (Moulton 1967:1406).

(4) Such a study brings into focus the manner in which varieties exploit the various distinctive features. Paris and Beauce use vowel quality to distinguish between (je)bois and (le)bois, but Burgundy uses vowel quantity in this case with /bwa/ versus /bwa:/. Burgundy has expanded the use of quantity for gender contrasts (ami, amie) and for grammatical contrasts (piquait, piquer, piquez).

(5) The use of a distinctive feature for a structural change. In closed syllables, Quebec has lax allophones for high vowels and, in addition, has retained vowel quantity as phonologically relevant feature. The addition of the

lax allophones has produced a 3 x 5 system, thereby making the phonetic interval between phonemes crucial. A valid hypothesis is that Quebec has solved this problem exactly as was done in Proto-French: diphthongization of long vowels, i.e. /e:/ in <u>maître</u> becomes [ei̯], /a:/ in <u>pâte</u> becomes [au̯], the /o:/ in <u>côte</u> becomes [ou̯]. This reduces the inventory to a 3 x 4 system:

```
i   ü   u
I   U   U
ɛ   œ   ɔ
    a
```

plus three diphthongs: ei̯, au̯, and ou̯. The question of the incipient phonologization of the lax high vowels makes this hypothesis all the more valid.[10]

NOTES

1. In presenting these tables, the conventions used by Martinet have been adopted: double lines separate nonneutralizable oppositions. When single lines are used, the opposition is less stable and some speakers may not maintain the contrast. If horizontal, single lines indicate contrasts in which quality is the distinctive feature. If vertical, the contrast is by quantity. The oblique line shows that the opposition is defined by a combination of quantity and quality.
2. Martinet (1971:213, 215, 217) also shows three <u>e</u>-phonemes for the Eastern sector, Normandy, and the Southwest. These areas tend to use distinctive quantity in a way that is analogous to Burgundy. Martinet believes that these regions show features, which were formerly typical of all the Northern half of France, but have receded before the advance of innovations from Paris.
3. Interesting speculation about the phonologization of these lax high vowels is occasioned by the occurrence of two English loan words: <u>clean</u> and <u>loose</u>. Both words have tense vowels in CVC and thus contrast with <u>machine</u> and <u>bouche</u>, which are regularly pronounced with <u>lax allophones</u>. The two loan words are so infrequent that it is probably better to regard them as examples of code switching.
4. Martinet (1971:214) says that 'Timbre et longueur entrent en jeu pour opposer les deux types de O, de Œ et de E, mais le rôle du timbre augmente d'importance en passant de E à Œ et de Œ à O ...'
5. Examples: pę̆na > Old French <u>pene</u>, Modern French <u>penne</u>, <u>panne</u>; <u>pēne</u> > <u>peine</u>, tēla > <u>teilə</u> > <u>toile</u>; auru > <u>ǫru</u> > <u>or</u>; <u>granu</u> > <u>graenu</u> > <u>grēnu</u> > <u>grain</u>; faba > <u>faevə</u> >

fə̄və > fève but, hĕri > ē̆ri > hier; bŏve > bŏ̄ve > buof > boeuf; flōre > flour > fleur.

6. The phoneme /r/ is apical in Beauce and, in the light of an analogous velarization of /a/ in part, one might ask whether parrain, as pronounced in Beauce, should not be phonemicized as having geminate r. One can also compare words like barrer 'close and lock', barrage 'dam'. So imbalanced is opposition between /-r-/ and /-rr-/ that the contrast may not be very stable (Moulton 1960:180f.).

7. The words with posterior a, listed by Grammont (1938: 26f.) are probably among those, which first showed the shift from [we] to [wA].

8. Cf. Massignon 1947, Haden 1948, Thogmartin 1969, Carrière 1941, Hall 1953, and Jourdain 1956.

9. We assume that words spelled with oi have the [wA] pronunciation.

10. Cf. Schogt 1968.

REFERENCES

Anglade, J. 1965. Grammaire élémentaire de l'ancien français. 3e tirage. Paris: Colin.
Brunot, F. et C. Bruneau. 1949. Précis de grammaire historique de la langue française. Paris: Masson.
Carrière, J. M. 1941. The phonology of Missouri French: A historical study. French Review 14.410-415; 510-515.
Conwell, M. and A. Juilland. 1963. Louisiana French grammar. (JL, series practica, 1). The Hague: Mouton.
Dauzat, A. 1928. Essais de géographie linguistique. 2e série: Problèmes phonétiques. Paris: Champion.
Ditchy, J. K. 1932. Les acadiens louisianais et leur parler. Paris-Baltimore-London: Droz-Hopkins-Oxford.
Fortier, A. 1891. The Acadians of Louisiana and their dialect. PMLA 6.1-33.
Galand, L. 1968. Timbre et longueur: les oppositions de voyelles dans une variété bourguignonne du français. Word 24.165-174.
Gendron, J. D. 1966. Tendances phonétiques du français parlé au Canada. Paris-Québec: Klincksieck-Laval.
Goodman, M. 1964. A comparative study of Creole French dialects. (JL, series practica, 4). The Hague: Mouton.
Grammont, M. 1938. Traité pratique de prononciation française. 9e édition. Paris: Delagrave.
Guilbeau, J. 1972. Folklore and the Louisiana lexicon. Louisiana Review 1.45-54.
Haden, E. 1948. La petite Cendrillouse: version acadienne de Cendrillon. Archives de Folklore 3.21-34.
Hall, R. A. 1953. Haitian Creole. American Anthropologist, 55. Memoir, 74.

Haudricourt, A. et A. Juilland. 1970. Essai pour une histoire structurale du phonétisme français. 2e édition révisée. (JL, series practica, 115). The Hague and Paris: Mouton.
Haudricourt, A. et J. M. C. Thomas. 1968. Les voyelles antérieures du parler parisien. Word 24.231-232.
Hull, A. 1955. The French spoken in Windsor, Ontario. Unpublished dissertation.
Jourdain, E. 1956. Le vocabulaire du parler créole de la Martinique. Paris: Klincksieck.
LaChaussée, F. de. 1974. Initiation à la phonétique historique de l'ancien français. Paris: Klincksieck.
Lane, G. 1934. Notes on Louisiana French, I. Language 10.323-333.
Lane, G. 1936. Notes on Louisiana French, II. Language 11.5-16.
Locke, W. N. 1949. Pronunciation of the French spoken at Brunswick, Maine. PADS, 12. Greensboro: ADS.
Martinet, A. 1946. Notes sur la phonologie du français vers 1700. Bulletin de la Soc. de Ling. de Paris 43.13-23.
Martinet, A. 1949. Phonology as functional phonetics. London: Oxford University.
Martinet, A. 1955. Economie des changements phonétiques. Berne: Francke.
Martinet, A. 1960. Eléments de linguistique générale. Paris: Colin.
Martinet, A. 1971. La prononciation du français contemporain. 2e éd. Genève: Droz.
Massignon, G. 1947. Les parlers français d'Acadie. French Review 21.45-53.
Morgan, R. 1959. Structural sketch of Saint Martin Creole. Anthropological Linguistics 1.20-29.
Morgan, R. 1970. Dialect leveling in non-English speech of Southwest Louisiana. Texas Studies in Bilingualism. Edited by G. Gilbert. 50-62. Berlin: de Gruyter.
Morgan, R. 1975. The regional French of County Beauce, Quebec. (JL, series practica, 177). The Hague and Paris: Mouton.
Moulton, W. J. 1960. The short vowel systems of Northern Switzerland. Word 16.155-182.
Moulton, W. J. 1967. Types of phonemic change. In: To honor Roman Jakobson. The Hague-Paris: Mouton. 1393-1407.
Moulton, W. J. 1968. The mapping of phonemic systems. Verhandlungen des 2. int. Dialektologenkongresses /1965/, II (=Zeitschrift für Mundartforschung, neue Folge, 4). 574-591.
Pope, M. K. 1952. From Latin to Modern French with especial consideration of Anglo-Normand. Second edition. Manchester: U. Press.

Reichstein, R. 1960. Etude des variations sociales et géographiques des faits linguistiques. Word 16.55-95.
Rheinfelder, H. 1953. Altfranzösische Grammatik. 2. Auflage. 5 Lieferungen. München: Max Hueber.
Saint-Jacques Fauqueroy, M. 1974. Guyanese: A French Creole. In: Pidgins and Creoles: Current trends and prospects. Edited by D. DeCamp and I. Hancock. Washington, D.C.: Georgetown University Press. 27-37.
Schogt, H. G. 1968. Une 'case vide': la phonologie diachronique du français canadien. Recherches sur la structure phonique du français canadien. Ed. par P. Léon. Montréal et Paris: Didier. 1-8.
Shorter Oxford English Dictionary. 1936. Rev. and ed. by C. T. Onions. 2nd ed. 2 vols. Oxford: Clarendon.
Sten, H. 1963. Manuel de phonétique française. 3e éd. Copenhagen: Munksgaard.
Thogmartin, C. 1968. French dialect of Old Mines, Missouri. Unpublished dissertation.
Troubetzkoy, N. S. 1949. Phonologie et géographie linguistique. Principes de phonologie, traduits par J. Cantineau, Appendice III. Paris: Klincksieck. 343-350.

COGNITIVE STYLES IN SPANISH AND ENGLISH

DOROTHY A. RISSEL
Indiana University, Bloomington

Folk definitions, or 'the explanations people give about the way they conceive of terms' (Mathiot 1974:2), have frequently been employed to investigate semantic relations used by native speakers of a language to organize and describe the meanings of lexical items. The question to which the current study addresses itself is one raised with regard to these definitions by Joseph Casagrande and Kenneth Hale in 1967. Are there significant differences in 'cognitive styles' of folk definitions, that is, in the types and degree to which different kinds of semantic relations are used in these definitions by speakers of different languages?

The situation which I felt would best lend itself to this type of investigation was a bilingual-bicultural one. For this reason, the lexical structure of the domain 'clothing' was selected for study among high-school age students representing the following communities: Non-Puerto-Rican English speakers from Buffalo, New York, Spanish-English bilinguals of Puerto Rican heritage living in Buffalo, and Spanish-speaking residents of Jayuya, Puerto Rico. These groups provided four linguistic data bases: (1) the English of monolinguals, (2) the English of bilinguals, (3) the Spanish of bilinguals living in a bicultural setting, and (4) the Spanish of near-monolinguals whose knowledge of English was minimal and who had never left Puerto Rico.

In the analysis of the domain, parallel procedures were followed with the three above-mentioned groups. In order to develop a representative inventory of terms, fifteen high-school age students from each community were asked to list all of the terms for articles of clothing they could recall in twenty minutes. Bilinguals were asked to respond on two separate occasions, once in English and once in Spanish. The inventories thus obtained were then personalized by two female students from each group who had agreed to participate in the in-depth studies.

In the next phase of the procedure, a folk definition for each term was elicited by asking the informants individually to respond to the question, 'What is a ____?' (Sp. ¿Qué es un/una ____?) with the name of the item under investigation filled in the blank. At this point, rather than proceeding with my own interpretation of the semantic relations expressed in these definitions, I asked the informants to assist in their identification. First, a list of questions which would re-elicit meaningful segments of each definition were developed by a trial-and-error process. For example, the folk definition for <u>blue jeans</u> supplied by a monolingual English-speaking informant, 'pants made out of denim', was segmented by using the following questions? 'What class of things do <u>blue jeans</u> belong to?', 'What kind of pants are <u>blue jeans</u>?' and, 'What are <u>blue jeans</u> made out of?'

On the basis of the foregoing procedure, an inventory of questions which would re-elicit all segments of the folk definitions was developed. The same inquiries were then made about each item under investigation to establish a full pattern of responses. The semantic relations obtaining in the set of responses to a given question were later identified by asking informants to explain the connection between their responses and the terms to which these pertained.

The purpose of involving the informants in the identification of these relations was to attempt to make the analysis correspond as closely as possible to their view of the meanings of the terms being investigated. In retrospect, I would say that a less biased view could have been obtained by employing a procedure suggested by Madeleine Mathiot (1974) wherein informants were asked to characterize folk definitions themselves by responding to the question 'What did you have in mind when you said that X is ____?' The informants' replies could then be utilized as the basis for formulating an appropriate question to re-elicit the desired semantic relation. I do contend, however, that the informant participation in the segmentation procedure used in the present study does reduce, to a certain degree, the investigator's analytic bias which so frequently pervades this type of study.

Before presenting the results of the study, I would like to emphasize that our original question regarding 'cognitive styles' in folk definitions encompassed both 'type' and 'degree of use' of semantic relations in these definitions. In answer to the question of type, I must say that the inventory of relations obtaining within the domain was essentially the same for all groups. These, with accompanying examples of illustrative folk definitions were:

(1) Synonymy
   body suit - 'the same as a body shirt'

(2) Class Inclusion
   (a) subordinate-to-superordinate
      blue jeans - 'pants made out of denim'
   (b) superordinate-to-subordinate
      camisa - 'hay camisas de vestir y camisas de estar por allí.' ('there are dress shirts and everyday shirts')

(3) Comparison
   la body shirt - '... es como un traje de baño, pero de tela, es como pantis también. ('It's like a bathing suit, but of cloth, it's like panties too')

(4) Properties
   (a) Fit
      body shirt - 'a shirt that fits close to the body'
   (b) Length
      knee socks - 'socks that come up to your knees'
   (c) Size
      bikini - 'a two-piece suit, very small'
   (d) Color
      camisilla - 'es blanca, ...' ('it's white')
   (e) Shape
      bow tie - 'a small piece of cloth in a bow that ...'

(5) Composition
   (a) Part-whole
      abrigo - 'uno lo usa en el invierno ..., some have zippers, otros tienen botones' ('one uses it in winter, ... some have zippers, others have buttons')
   (b) Material
      blue jeans - 'pants made out of denim'

(6) Setting
   bata - 'se utiliza mucho en casa ...' ('it's used a lot at home')

(7) Arrangement
   undershirt - 'kind of underwear that goes on the top part of the body'

(8) Go-together
   blusa - 'La blusa se pone con la falda' ('a blouse is worn with a skirt')

(9) People-associated
   calzoncillos - 'los usan los hombres ...' ('men wear them ...')

(10) Function
   bufanda - 'se usa para abrigar la garganta ...' ('it's used to protect the throat ...')

(11) Manipulation
   bow tie - '... it ties in a bow'

Only with regard to two of these relations, Class Inclusion and Comparison, were any differences among the groups discovered.

First, let us examine these two relations. Both of them differ from the other relations operating within the domain in the sense that folk definitions which express either relation are frequently accompanied by a statement of differentiation based on one of the other relations. For example, the folk definition for blue jeans, listed above, classifies them as pants and differentiates them from other members of the class on the basis of their composition--'made of denim'. In the definition of undershirt ((7) above), the Arrangement relation is also used as a differentiator. Likewise, Composition is used in the Comparison definition ((3) above) to distinguish between body shirt and bathing suit.

These two relations differ, however, with regard to the existence of a superordinate-subordinate relation between the terms defined. Class Inclusion implies that this relation does exist between two terms. That is, one is a 'kind of' the other. Class Inclusion was used in the folk definitions in one of two ways: either (a) two or more subordinate items that are 'kinds of' the one under consideration were specified (shirts and blouses are both kinds of tops), or (b) the superordinate term of which the item being defined is a kind was given (a shrink is a kind of top). It was this second pattern of Class Inclusion that frequently was accompanied in the definitions by a statement of differentiation.

Although Comparison definitions are similar to ones of Class Inclusion in that they often include a statement of differentiation, the superordinate-subordinate element is missing. These definitions imply only that two items are similar, not that one is a 'kind of' the other. An example of this type of definition is listed in (3) above.

As observed by Harold Conklin (1962), Comparisons are frequently made between members of the same class. This was sometimes the case in the present data. However, the following types of Comparisons not involving two members of the same class were also discovered:

(1) Items that could not be classified as belonging to either of two large subcategories were treated in terms of Comparisons. For example, culottes were considered by informants to be neither a kind of pants, nor a kind of skirt, but similar to both.
(2) Items such as la body shirt ('a body shirt') and el traje de baño ('bathing suit') which are members of two different subcategories were compared.

Now that the differences between Class Inclusion and Comparison have been discussed, let us look at the ways in which they were employed by Spanish and English speakers.

The most apparent contrast was in the frequency of use of these relations in the folk definitions. The subordinate-superordinate class-inclusive definition accompanied by a statement of differentiation within the class was favored, by far, over the comparative type by monolingual English speakers. The ratio for one informant was 1.8 to 1, and for the other 2.7 to 1. Spanish speakers from Jayuya, on the other hand, favored Comparisons over subordinate-to-superordinate Class Inclusion with an accompanying statement of differentiation in proportions of 2.47 to 1 and 7.4 to 1. If simple statements of Class Inclusion with no accompanying differentiators are counted, these ratios are reduced to 1.28 to 1 and 1.05 to 1. Overall, however, Comparisons were used 1.5 to 2.6 times more frequently by Spanish speakers in Jayuya than they were by non-Puerto Rican English speakers in Buffalo. The bilinguals, though employing both types of definitions to a lesser degree than either group of monolinguals, did follow similar patterns. That is, they favored Comparison when responding in Spanish and showed an increased preference for Class Inclusion in English.

We can, then, answer 'yes' to part of our original question. A difference in frequency of use of certain relations was, indeed, found in this study, even though differences in the inventory of relations were not.

The second phase of the study went beyond the mere analysis of the semantic relations present in folk definitions. In it, informants were asked to place each term under investigation in a more inclusive class. It was here that even more striking contrasts between English and Spanish were discovered.

English speakers, when asked to perform the classification task, usually replied with a term of a lower level of

specificity. For example, <u>pantyhose</u> were classified as a
'kind of' <u>stockings</u>, and <u>stockings</u> were grouped as a 'kind
of' <u>underwear</u>. Similarly, <u>hot pants</u> were grouped as a 'kind
of' <u>shorts</u>, which were in turn classified as a 'kind of'
<u>pants</u>. There were, however, a small number of general sub-
class-labeling terms beyond which English speakers would
cease to categorize. Terms of low specificity such as <u>coat</u>,
<u>top</u>, and <u>pants</u> were never voluntarily placed in a broader
category by these informants. Furthermore, there was a
very high percentage of agreement (66%) between the two
monolingual English speakers on the labeling of the less
specific class for all items in the study.
   Spanish speakers, on the other hand, did not rely exclusively on the subordinate-to-superordinate form of expressing Class Inclusion. Certainly, there were some cases of
it. For example, <u>los mamelucos</u> ('bib-overalls'), <u>los hot
pants</u>, and <u>los mahones</u> ('blue jeans') were all categorized
as 'tipos de pantalón' ('kinds of pants'). However, statements of Class Inclusion of this kind account for slightly
less than half of the informants' responses. Numerous
items were classified as being similar to or belonging to
the same subclass as items of which they are not a kind.
For example, '<u>la estola</u> se da parecida <u>al poncho</u> ('a shawl
is similar to a <u>poncho</u>'), 'el <u>jacket</u> es parecido al <u>suéter</u>'
('a <u>jacket</u> is similar to a <u>sweater</u>'). Other items were
grouped as belonging to classes formed on the basis of criteria that were dimensions of one of the other semantic relations operating within the domain. That is, the dimension
'sex of the wearer' that underlies the relation 'People-
Associated' was used to form a class in the following: <u>la
camisa</u> ('shirt'), <u>la corbata</u> ('tie') and <u>el gabán</u> ('suit
jacket') were all placed in the category 'la vestimenta del
hombre' ('men's clothing'); <u>la falda</u> ('skirt') was classified
as 'la vestimenta de la mujer' ('women's clothing'). Likewise, Function was frequently employed in this manner. For
example, <u>chinelas</u> ('slippers') were placed in the group
'cosas que se usan para dormir' ('things used for sleeping').
   In this phase of the study we have seen that monolingual
English speakers consistently classified terms for articles
of clothing with regard to a small number of superordinate
terms, while Spanish speakers employed several systems of
classification, one parallel to English and the others
available in English but rarely employed.
   Some very interesting parallel patterns emerged in the
interviews with bilinguals. One informant, who was observed
to be heavily Spanish dominant, consistently formed classes
on the basis of relational criteria both in Spanish and
English. For example, <u>el coat</u>, <u>el abrigo</u> (alternate terms
for 'coat' with slight contrasts in meaning) and <u>la suera</u>

('sweater') were all categorized as something used for winter ('cosas que se usan para el invierno'); a blouse as 'something women wear'. However, the other informant who seemed to be equally fluent in both languages, while favoring the types of classifications most frequently observed in Jayuya, could apply the superordinate class-labeling pattern, used to the exclusion of all others in English to Spanish when asked to do so. This informant was very hesitant in performing this task, however, and frequently remarked that it seemed more correct to label the class in English. It would seem then, that while the various patterns discussed are more common to one language than the other, there is nothing that prohibits bilinguals from applying either of these patterns to either of their codes.

In conclusion, it can first be stated that a preference in cognitive style as defined by Casagrande and Hale was found in the folk definitions supplied by the informants who participated in the present study. It has been demonstrated that, at least among the small sample of speakers interviewed within a limited age group, there is a difference in frequency of use of Comparison and in the manner of expressing Class Inclusion.

Secondly, we have observed that when asked specifically to perform the task of classification, English speakers grouped with regard to a limited number of terms of low specificity, while Spanish speakers employed this pattern in addition to several others. We may conclude, therefore, that we are not dealing as much with frequency of occurrence as we are with alternate modes of assigning class membership and organizing terms within a domain in relation to one another.

Certainly, the ability of bilinguals to work with either system and to apply the preferred pattern from one of their languages to the other dissuades us from making any claims of linguistic determinism. Rather, we would prefer to search for the cause of these differences within the cultures in which these languages are spoken.

A contrast which immediately brings itself to mind is an urban-rural one. The non-Puerto-Rican English speakers interviewed in Buffalo, natives of a city of approximately 463,000, definitely represented an urban culture. On the other hand, the Spanish speakers from Jayuya, a small town of less than 10,000, came from a rural background. The bilinguals in Buffalo function daily in a situation in which two cultures are in contact. Their environment is in some facets English-speaking and urban, and in others Spanish-speaking and, according to an informal survey taken during the course of this study, rural in origin.

Another area which warrants further investigation is the possible relation between the results of the current study and the 1974 work of Manuel Ramírez III and Alfredo

Castañeda with Anglo- and Mexican-American children. These authors found that the former group tended to perceive in a field-independent manner, that is, they respond to events or objects independently of field or context, while their Mexican-American peers tended to be field sensitive, responding to events or objects as fused with their surroundings. Furthermore, Ramírez, Casteñeda, et al. (1974) found these differences to be directly related to traditional values in child rearing. Children who grew up in traditional homes were discovered to be much more field sensitive than those from nontraditional families.

Before concluding, a word of caution is needed. Ramírez, Castañeda, and the present author all refer to the phenomena they study as cognitive styles. However, the term is being employed in different ways. In the current study, it refers to the manner of use of semantic relations in folk definitions after Casagrande and Hale (1967). Ramírez and Castañeda, on the other hand, define cognitive styles in the psychological sense, that is, the manner in which people perceive and their way of processing information. The connection between the two remains unclear, but the apparent similarities certainly warrant further investigation.

REFERENCES

Casagrande, Joseph B. and Kenneth L. Hale. 1967. Semantic relationships in Papago folk definitions. In: Studies in Southwest ethnology. Edited by Hymes and Bittle. The Hague: Mouton. 165-193.
Conklin, Harold C. 1962. Lexicographical treatment of folk taxonomies. Reprinted in: Cognitive Anthropology. Edited by Stephen A. Tyler. New York: Holt, Rinehart, and Winston. 41-59.
Mathiot, Madeleine. 1974. Cognitive styles in color terminology. Paper read at the 73rd Annual Meeting of the American Anthropological Association.
Ramírez III, Manuel and Alfredo Casteñeda. 1974. Cultural democracy, bicognitive development, and education. New York: Academic Press.
Ramírez III, Manuel, Alfredo Casteñeda, et al. 1974. Introduction to cognitive styles. ERIC ED 108 497.

CONSIDERATIONS OF THE ENGLISH AND HOME SUBDIALECT ENVIRONMENTS FOR THE TEACHING OF SPANISH TO SPANISH-DOMINANT BILINGUAL CHILDREN

MORDECAI RUBIN
Teachers College, Columbia University

The recent dramatic growth of Hispanic populations and bilingual education programs in the United States has given rise to a new category of Spanish-language teaching environment--'native' Spanish classes, a phenomenon already sufficiently widespread to have occasioned the sobriquet 'N classes'. In view of the pressures--and rewards--associated with academic publishing, it is not surprising that materials and methodological guidelines have begun pouring forth before analysis, discussion, and longitudinal studies have been able to clarify what is new and what is old in the needs, attitudes, and capacities of these 'native' language students. In the many high school programs I have observed, two approaches are popular, both predicated upon intuitive analogy: (1) one view holds that 'N' students are merely further along than their traditional English-background counterparts and simply require advanced, sophisticated texts. We may call this the 'high-level' approach. (2) Another interpretation suggests that language materials written in this country are fundamentally misoriented with respect to 'N' classes and that materials should be sought in the school systems of Puerto Rico and other Spanish-speaking countries--in several cases, even Spain. This might be termed the 'home culture' approach.

If we assume that the fundamental aspiration of our educational system is to prepare and equip young people to fulfill their potential and function happily from an initial base in this society, we cannot be content with either of the approaches just described. Whether we think of the graduates of our bilingual programs as slithering into the famous mainstream of United States society or prefer to think of them as tenaciously championing their minority heritage in those picturesque urban enclaves we call barrios, or ghettos, we surely agree that our instructional philosophy must take into account at least two of the linguistic environments in which 'N' students function continually, to wit: (1) the English language of the majority society and (2) the Spanish spoken in the students' homes and neighborhoods.

Our search for a considered and balanced approach to 'N' classes will begin, then, by examining the analogies implicit in the high level and home culture approaches. Clearly, 'native' Hispanic students share with their English-background schoolmates the need to expand their repertoire of Spanish structures and lexical items as well as the capacity to grow in insight, broadmindedness, sensitivity, and imaginativeness via their tentative tiptoeings into the alter world of literature.

But whereas the use of Spanish is, for the English-background student, somewhat exotic, or at least an extra skill, it is for the 'N' student an element of his identity, of his relationships with peers and with subculture adults; it is even, as we might expect, a factor in his self-esteem. In the matter of learning level, 'N' students cannot be treated as though the home and the street have taken care of the elementary stage. To be sure, we must not disregard, nor fail to take advantage of, the 'N' student's being at ease in Spanish and having some knowledge of the language. But that knowledge cannot be graphed at any single locus on the learning line of the English-background student in the system. The native student's command of Spanish is inconsistent and without the hierarchical organization that helps the nonnative student improve and expand what he learns. The 'N' student's ultra-practical adeptness at periphrastic manipulation and word borrowing weakens his motivation for augmenting his Spanish lexical repertoire and more often than not turns out to be antithetical to that self-consciousness in speech that discerns the patterns upon which we build and analogize in language study. Furthermore, it is not easy to evaluate and cope with the significant gap in 'N' students between the resources for spontaneous linguistic emission and the fuller repertoire that is evoked for the receptor or comprehension mode.

Yet while the native students are not to be viewed as advanced versions of nonnative students, neither can they be dealt with as though we were all in another country. The cultural weighting of educational materials from another society can only be of the spottiest relevance here; and the pedagogical tenets underlying much such material may well be

at variance with the teacher in the classroom, as well as
with the orientation of other courses and experiences provided by the system here.

In addition, we need to exercise caution in the intensification of Hispanic 'authenticity' in the world of 'N'
classes, since one of the most lamented side-effects of
current programs in bilingual education has been the polari-
zation of students into Hispanic and Anglo cliques, an
ironic development in the context of brotherhood and unity-
in-pluralism that have been prominent in the rhetoric es-
pousing bilingual education. Furthermore, the use of text
programs from other countries often imposes upon us ready-
made decisions about dialect and regionalisms that are more
properly worked out here, at the source of instruction. It
may, of course, be argued that local materials similarly
reflect the views and decisions of text writers. True, but
it is generally much more feasible to examine and compare a
substantial variety of materials in the local market. I
feel no hesitation in including Spanish or Latin American
text materials in the competition; my quarrel is with the
a priori assumption of virtue and appropriateness of such
materials for teaching Spanish-dominant bilingual students
in the United States.

The foregoing considerations explain, in part, why 'N'
classes are not very popular assignments among the many
Spanish teachers with whom I have had direct and indirect
contact; but they are only tangential to the primary focus
of this discussion--the question of Spanish dialects and
the **native** classroom. This is not a topic of idle inquiry
nor solely an area of research interest for linguists and
teachers. I have had occasion to conduct a dozen or so in-
tensive Spanish courses for adults over the past decade and
I am still searching for the proper combination of quip and
administrative sobriety with which to answer the recurrent
question, 'Are we going to learn Puerto Rican Spanish or
the other kind?' (I assume 'the other kind' to be a sort of
Spanish Spanish for Spaniards.)

A few years back, when the New School for Social Research
in New York City advertised a practical and timely course
for adults, described as teaching New York Puerto Rican
Spanish, complete with Spanglish, it seemed to generate
some local interest--at least enough for several bombs to
be thrown. Reactions such as these certainly contributed
to the widespread feeling in linguistic circles a few years
back that the term 'dialect' should be avoided altogether,
much as the United Nations discarded the term 'under-
developed nations' in favor of the less provocative terminology 'developing nations'. We need not tarry on the term
'dialect', its 19th century deprecatory connotation, and

the attempts of 20th century linguists to employ it dispassionately. Let us ask simply, 'What kind of Spanish should we try to teach to Spanish-dominant bilingual students?'

Fishman and Lueders-Salmon (1972) point out that Americans are unique in even considering teaching home and neighborhood varieties of speech as the standard in the classroom. But, in fairness, this observation may be more germane to teaching a national language to domestic speakers of subdialects. The teaching of Spanish to a Hispanic student population in an English-speaking society is a somewhat different question. In any case we cannot blithely accept generalized models from abroad--leeches and blood-letting were once quite universal.

It might be pointed out, at this juncture, that the inevitable comparison with the teaching of Standard English to speakers of Black English is rather spurious, in view of two fundamental differences between the linguistic situations and attitudes of the Black and Hispanic minority communities. (1) There is less difference between Barrio Spanish and Standard Spanish than between Black and Standard English. (2) The Hispanic community has a shorter history of residence and suffering in the United States and does not resentfully champion Barrio street Spanish as an independent language parallel to the standard variety. One finds no popular community support for the asseveration of a few linguists that the barrio patterns should be fostered and will one day yield a new and valuable language.

The following dialogue is quoted from Fishman's exhaustive interviews with Spanish-dominant high school students (1968):

Fishman: Tell me about talking Spanish to teachers in high school. Do you try to talk better when you're talking to them?
Mike: I guess we all try.
Tommy: Yeah.

Fishman then asked about popular versus formal Spanish.

Tommy: I think both are necessary, because when you speak to adults or parents you speak formal Spanish; but when you speak to a friend or someone you know really well, you speak in familiar Spanish.

All the youngsters reported difficulty in speaking formal Spanish; all reported feeling the need for formal Spanish in various circumstances. I do not consider high school students the best arbiters of curriculum; but it would seem only reasonable to suggest--from this interchange--that the teaching of the standard dialect of Spanish would be a sound contribution to the education of at least these students.

I believe that this question has been unnecessarily complicated by some writers in applied linguistics today. Pendulitis being the natural affliction of dedicated theoreticians, it is not surprising that the 19th century praise-and-damnation system for categorizing differences between speech communities should be succeeded by a democratic acceptance of, and interest in, all linguistic variation. In fairness, it must be acknowledged that many writers--Fries himself, Robert Allen more recently (1971)--have insisted on the validity of all varieties of speech only within the context in which they function successfully--and solely--for everyday communication. But this caveat is often lost in the rush for equality. As egalitarian as we may be, we cannot honestly abandon all notion of a prestige dialect and somewhat measurable distances between that dialect and others, respectively, this distance correlating broadly with intelligibility across regional boundaries.

That the passion for dethroning the prestige dialect and enshrining practicality and de factoism as acceptance criteria should have spilled over into areas of curriculum, materials writing, and even classroom staffing may be attributed, I suggest, to the projection of our own interests. That is, since applied linguists are generally linguists first, and appliers secondarily, it is entrely likely that our own joy at witnessing adstratum interplay, linguistic borrowing, κοινή evolution, and that fascinating code-switching that intrigued Weinreich and many others since has influenced our thinking on educational questions. For indeed, this is more an educational than a linguistic matter; and our discussion would not be complete without some brief reflections on the purpose of education and, specifically, the proper objectives for the teacher of the native Spanish class.

The normal Spanish word for school education is not <u>educación</u> but <u>preparación</u>. Preparation for what? We cannot be certain at the high school level, and we know that differences will be legion in the future life styles of our students. Yet every high-minded teacher is a surrogate for that adult that must one day emerge from today's restless student and take a place among men. The thoughtful teacher of any subject will be interested in helping keep options open and in equipping students with the skills and the attitudes that will give them the most flexibility, the greatest freedom of choice in their adult lives.

Educators still speak today of the centrality of personal discovery in the proper learning experience, discovery to which the student is led by the skillful teacher. As far back as 1903, Hildebrand, speaking of teaching standard dialect German, enjoined that 'the teacher of German should not teach things that pupils can find out for themselves' (Fishman and Lueders-Salmon 1972). I would amend that to read 'that students will find out for themselves', but the point is well taken. In the case of our 'N' classes, we hardly need a sophisticated instructional program to teach Juan how to talk to his mother or to his friends on the street. He will manage that. It is not present peer conformity but rather future social mobility that should concern us. It is a dismal education indeed that only illuminates the ghetto child's reality rather than intimating that a sweeter reality exists and may one day be attained. It is a misguided education that cultivates skills and styles that will forever anchor the student, if not imprison him, in the barrio rather than furnishing at least the linguistic habiliments appropriate to knocking on higher doors, even within the Hispanic community.

We need not travel far to find examples of handicapping through dialect restriction. I can offer a frightening example--admittedly extreme, but not exaggerated in the recounting: an unusual case of child 'retardation' came to our attention not too long ago. The child's speech was profuse but unintelligible, and the decision had been made to institutionalize him. Out of curiosity, a linguist on our staff requested a tape recording of the child's speech. The recording--slowed down and studied--proved to be nothing more than a record of speech in Puerto Rican street Spanish, delivered with the phonological patterns of Harlem Black English!

Of course, there are special problems involved in teaching a kind of Spanish that is not quite the daily idiom in the student's home. There will be the occasional machismo, whereby a father is discomfited by the prospect of his son being educated to deviate from or 'surpass' the father; and there will be that amusing phenomenon I term abuelismo. Abuelo is Spanish for grandfather, and abuelismo is operant when Juan arrives in class insisting, 'Mi abuelo says it this way!' But these are interaction challenges for the teacher: how to inculcate attitudes about the language that will obviate clashes with uneducated or antieducational elements. Training for such problems would not be out of place in the background of Spanish teachers for 'N' classes but need not be explored further here.

The teacher, of course, must be aware that teaching the standard dialect is not tantamount to overlying the spontaneous vernacular of 'N' students, and that it is not especially difficult to make clear the difference between sporadic eruptions of undifferentiated--and often emotional --vernacular communication and the attentive study of a target dialect. The students are already aware of some distinction between levels, even within their vernacular. I have found no student really oblivious to the level of seriousness and refinement reflected in such everyday usages as 'Vaya, brother', 'Cógelo suave, man'.

'N' students can understand the concept of modes of speech for different contexts, universal norms, and the possibility of being conscious of the kind of language one is speaking at a given moment. The idea of good impression forms and more careful phonation for formal circumstances can easily replace the old right-wrong opposition. And we must bear in mind that **Standard** Spanish is subliminally legitimized for almost every person in the barrio by movies, television, radio, and public advertising.

All of this can lead students to a heightened awareness of societal criteria for oral language alternatives, to care and purpose in code selection (and sustaining), and finally, even to a basic appreciation of language styles and aesthetics. More will be said of this further on, in connection with the question of literature in 'N' classes.

Let me offer a sampling of the kinds of problems that may be addressed in 'N' classes, particularly at the most advanced level: I pass over the obvious considerations of Hispanicized English items replacing Spanish words. You are all familiar with rufo and toile, chequear and trustear. And, of course, we would expect false cognates to turn honest: realizar, casualmente, principal, eventualmente. Somewhat more confusing is the literal translation of English idioms: tirar fuera for 'to throw out', llamar para atrás meaning 'to call back', cógelo suave, 'take it easy'.

Perhaps the most subtle influence of English in the barrio Spanish that shows up in 'N' classes is the interference that produces frequency distortion. For example, English revels in passive constructions; Spanish permits them but with reluctance and with important restrictions. 'N' students employ the passive at least twice as often as is natural in Spanish (where impersonal active constructions are much preferred). This is particularly ungainly--as well as traditionally incorrect--in the present tense of action verbs. Sentences like 'Esto no es vendido en esta tienda' are English in disguise. Similarly, the present continuous or progressive, which is the only accurate form for the majority of English verbs of action when expressing the immediate, transpiring present, exists in Spanish as a secondary present tense structure, available for variation and emphasis. Barrio speakers characteristically overuse the progressive and neglect the simple present that predominates in **Standard** Spanish. They also extend the imitation of the English progressive to such colossal formulations as 'Ya me estoy yendo' or '¿Estas viniendo con nosotros?' which fly in the face of fundamental restrictions on the use of the progressive in Spanish.

The selection of **Standard** Spanish as the dialect to be taught to barrio children corresponds to the deepest ambitions of the Hispanic community and rather than threatening their identity, appends to their local stature a minimal cosmopolitan component that ties them to the culture and literature of all Spanish-speaking countries. In this connection, a few particular observations are in order on the selection of literature for the native Spanish class.

The modish passion for the vernacular led one of my colleagues to assert, in a paper at the 1975 MLA meetings (Milán 1975) that **the writings of certain barrio poets constitute admirable literature for bilingual classes,** since they incorporate much street idiom and depict the seamiest side of Hispanic life in New York, things familiar and real to our bilingual students.

How sad! Is it not a function of literature to be uplifting? Is not contact with literature supposed to fertilize young imaginations? And in language classes in particular, what can rival good literature for demonstrating the impact and effectiveness of elegant language, render attractive a variety of language that is no more than one extreme of the graded continuum, at the other end of which stands barrio slang? Must our barrio children be deprived of this skylight in the cupola because of our linguistic interest in the most colloquial varieties of language?

There are things familiar and real to our students beyond the thundering subway, dirty streets, and sweaty armpits of verismo verse from the barrio. There are matters of the human condition that are touched upon in most good art and that can awaken interest and identification in the jauntiest macho of our high school 'N' classes.

An illustrative anecdote: There is an old public high school in the Bronx; its student population of over four thousand includes many Hispanics. The school--including its 'N' classes--is not noted for its elevated academic ambiance; streetwear and transistor radios are more typical of its classrooms than are editions of Cervantes.

A new teacher there was assigned several 'N' classes and asked my advice on the teaching of both language and literature for these groups. In particular, she was interested in trying something special on the occasion of being observed by the **department head.** My suggestion for the day was a poem by Octavio Paz called La Calle. The piece deals with the uneasy situation of being followed down a dark street--being followed, following (the familiar espejismo), all confusing and illusory, somehow symbolic.

Initially the young teacher (and subsequently the **department head**) were stunned by the idea; but after we worked out motivation, identification, points of language, and the rest, the experiment was undertaken, complete with my own theatrical reading on a cassette. Results were nothing less than marvelous. And by the end of the period, when the teacher asked mysteriously what 'else' the <u>calle</u> 'street' might represent ('Poets often mean a lot more than they say!'), a towering footballish young man--replete with street jacket and visored cap--waved his hand frantically ... 'Missy, missy, ¡esa calle es la vida!'

REFERENCE

Fishman, Joshua, and Erika Lueders-Salmon. 1972. What has the sociology of language to say to the teacher? On teaching the standard variety to speakers of dialectal or sociolectal varieties. In: Functions of language in the classroom. Edited by John Cazden and Dell Hymes. New York: Teachers College Press. 67-83.

A LINGUISTIC TYPOLOGY OF DICTIONARIES:
WITH REFERENCE TO FRENCH

GLADYS E. SAUNDERS
Pennsylvania State University

0. I shall begin by reviewing briefly the efforts of other specialists, in particular those of Y. Malkiel, B. Quemada, J. Rey-Debove, and A. Rey. Afterwards, I shall provide some information on the dominant types of lexical activity which have evolved in France during the last five centuries. Then I shall put forth an attractive typology of dictionaries, based on what I call intersecting linguistic 'universal' and linguistic 'genetic' features. Finally, I shall comment upon the internal structure of one very recent type of French dictionary--one not yet discussed elsewhere in the literature, yet particularly enlightening for the subject at hand. But first a word about the concept of dictionary.

Since the term 'dictionary' is not really linguistically significant (dictionaries, as we know, are sometimes camouflaged behind incomprehensible or delusive titles), and since the definitions assigned to the term are **multifarious** and can include everything from highly specialized lexicographical texts to glossaries, word-indexes, alphabetical lists of names, places, insects, and the like, I have decided to follow, for the purposes of this study, the advice suggested by J. Rey-Debove (1971), namely that we list certain characteristic features which define the concept of 'dictionary', and then group all of the existing lexical studies as dictionaries (if they possess the specified features) or **nondictionaries (if they do not possess the speci-**fied features). Accordingly, she recognizes the following as being characteristic features of the dictionary: (a) didacticism, (b) the separable characteristic of the messages which compose it, (c) their independent readability, (d) the structural characteristic of the described units taken collectively, (e) the presence of information on the units as signs

(<u>signifiants</u> and <u>signifiés</u>). I find this characterization or delimitation of the concept of dictionary linguistically quite adequate.

1. Several specialists have on various occasions talked about dictionary typology. Malkiel (1959, 1960), to my knowledge, was the first to consider a typology of dictionaries on the basis of distinctive features. The question he raises is this: '[Is it] legitimate to regard a reference book as a bundle of characteristic features which could be reassembled in some kind of arrangement that might be expressed in a simple formula?' (1960:4). Malkiel does not give us the simple formula but he does believe that his work affords us the means of constructing it. Illustrating with a corpus of Spanish lexical texts, he proposes three classificatory criteria: 'range', 'perspective', and 'presentation'. Classification by 'range' includes the volume and spread of the nomenclature, the number of languages involved, and the degree of concentration on purely lexical data. Classification by 'perspective' includes the diachronic versus synchronic dimension, the contrasting patterns of arrangement (e.g. alphabetic versus semantic), and the contrasting levels of tone. Classification by 'presentation' concerns the presence of verbal documentation (observed discourse), on the one hand, and graphic illustrations (nonlinguistic information), on the other. There are obviously problems with Malkiel's typology. For example, he mixes oppositions that are very different, and posits subtypes which appear to be unusable or which offer scarcely any typological interest (e.g. classification by levels of tone).

While recognizing, and rightly so, the importance of Malkiel's contribution to the inventory of criteria for analysis, Quemada (1968:23) explains that the relative failure of this attempt appears to demonstrate the difficulty of reducing dictionaries in the manner of phonemes of a linguistic system to distinctive features. Indeed, in the historical optic in which **Quemada** places himself, the difficulty could be insurmountable. He considers a vast body of lexical texts (French, or partially French), published between the dates of 1539 and 1863, so varied in tendencies (many of which are not even classifiable as 'dictionary', in accordance with the definition cited) that one could only establish concrete types of utilization, undefinable by any set of simple traits of a general nature, as Malkiel suggested. After having challenged the possibility of a classification on the basis of distinctive features, Quemada selects an approach that is more historical (i.e. phenomenological) and methodological. He, like Malkiel, utilizes three classificatory criteria. The first concerns the nature of the dictionary text according to whether it originates from one or from several linguistic systems. The second corresponds to the level of semantic analysis and to the nature of the information. The third concerns the extension of the information, which encompasses almost every aspect of lexicography, and depends rather closely on the choice of a **sociocultural model of utilization.** Quemada's typology certainly responds to his objective, which is to analyze a vast corpus of French dictionaries as they relate to historical events. And with this, one cannot take issue.

Josette Rey-Debove (1971) is concerned with contemporary French dictionaries and limits her study to five fairly homogeneous works, the structure of which she studies in depth. She is not so much interested in establishing an abstract, general classification of dictionary types as she is in analyzing the semiotic and linguistic aspects of certain specified dictionaries and in studying the practice of encoding and decoding lexicographic messages. In this field she makes a remarkable contribution.

Inspired by the works of Josette Rey-Debove and Nina Catach, Alain Rey attempts to extract from a rather reduced number of dictionaries the most general analysis possible. The genetic typology that he proposes does not compete with previous classifications, nor does it render the same services. While previous typologies attempted to separate the texts of dictionaries according to overlapping criteria, all on the same plane, Rey proposes an abstract model based on a hierarchical classification of the dictionary texts. The model comprises a reasonable number (7) of digital theories --rather crude in presentation and difficult to follow--which the author summarizes in appended tables. These allow one to establish the formula desired by Malkiel. Rey's classification is impressive, but complex. He admits that while it is insufficient to handle the extraordinary variety of lexical texts, such as those studied by Quemada, it at least uncovers some fundamental oppositions, and thereby serves to define better the paths and means to complex metalinguistic practice. The typology that I propose is perhaps different from the above mentioned studies in that it is a composite of all of them. It attempts to be universal, general, and abstract, while at the same time claiming to be genetic, specific, and concrete. But before discussing it further, we must take inventory of our data.

2. If one studies the distribution of French dictionaries along a time axis, as I originally set out to do (before learning that **Quemada** had already covered the territory quite thoroughly), one ascertains that certain works cluster around certain dates. The dictionaries that I shall mention are considered as representatives of particular types. It

will be assumed that all other dictionaries (defined as such by the characterization just specified) fall into one of these types.

Chronologically speaking, the sixteenth century is representative of the plurilingual type of dictionary. Credit must be given to Robert Estienne for having created, in a sense, French lexicography. His first lexicographic compendium (le <u>Dictionnaire francais</u>: <u>latin, autrement dit les Mots francais avec les manieres d'user d'iceux</u>), in which the French language took priority (over Latin) was published around 1539. The title of his work contains for the first time the word <u>dictionnaire</u> (derived etymologically from the Latin <u>dictio</u>, meaning 'word' and 'diction'). Numerous studies have been made of Estienne's <u>Dictionnaire</u>, which in actuality is only a translation of his <u>Thesaurus</u> (published eight years earlier). For our purposes, we need only reiterate that Estienne's work was extremely important for the incentive that it had on vocabulary studies of the period. Its weakness, however, was in the selection of nomenclature. Estienne selected the nomenclature from certain literary (Latin) authors, and then attempted to establish a French nomenclature according to the function of Latin words. Thus, his dictionary does not reflect contemporary sixteenth century usage. Definitions, as such, did not exist. The sample entries shown below are typical:

(1) <u>oiseau</u>, AUIS, VOLUCRIS.
   petit <u>oiseau</u>, AUICULA.
(2) <u>peindre</u>, vient de PINGERE, par mutation de <u>g</u> en <u>d</u>.
   Par quoy semble qu'on deburoit escrire <u>pindre</u>, et a ce retire assez notre prononciation.

Quemada (1968) observed that more dictionaries were not written in the sixteenth century because the meaning of words was not fixed. The classic example is the famous French author, Rabelais, who possessed an enormous vocabulary and who would readily coin new words, but without consideration for their semantic precision. According to his own personal whim, he would use first one synonym and then another; or he would assign a single word on the same page two different meanings. Since a clear-cut distinction between the arts and sciences did not exist in the sixteenth century, as we establish today, the dictionary could not define a word that was used more often than not according to individual capriciousness or pure chance. Obviously, the lexicographer cannot compose a dictionary before word usage has been fixed and before some order has been established in the lexical system. (One should also recall that in the Middle Ages French had been considered as a language inferior to Latin and that all lexical works were viewed from a Latin perspective. This tradition was carried over into the sixteenth century.)

One other dictionary of this period should be mentioned: one which is sometimes wrongly presented as the first entirely French (monolingual) dictionary to be published, when actually, it is linked almost directly to Estienne's bilingual dictionary. Here I refer to the lexicographical work of Nicot, <u>le Tresor</u> (<u>Tresor de la langue francaise, tant ancienne que moderne auquel entre autres choses sont les mots propres de marine, venerie et fauconnerie</u>), in which the author offers to his readers Latin equivalents. Nicot's work is more complete than the other dictionaries of the sixteenth century: it offers explanations on the meanings of words, on the orthography, gender, etymology, etc.

With the seventeenth century, lexicographical research takes a new bent. This is the period which gave rise to the modern monolingual dictionary and to the application of social norms to lexical items. Three dictionaries, similar in type should be mentioned: Richelet's <u>Dictionnaire français</u> (1680), Furetière's <u>Dictionnaire de l'Académie</u> (1690), and <u>le Dictionnaire de l'Académie</u> (1694)--the last of which is generally characterized by its omissions. Among the omissions cited in the Preface are: archaic words, popular words, neologisms, specialized terms (i.e. trade terms, scientific terms, artistic terms, etc.), and terms of comportment. Furthermore, this particular dictionary is often criticized for its numerous inaccuracies of definitions. Also, lexical entries are arranged according to the order of the etymological root instead of the formal arrangement by alphabetic order. (Within the root morphemes, however, the alphabetic order is followed.) Arrangement according to etymological roots, while offering the advantage of reflecting the history of the word, proved to be of little practical use in the seventeenth century when etymological and semantic studies were still in the beginning stage.

The eighteenth century marks a deviation in the dictionary tradition. It founds the encyclopedia and encyclopedic dictionary, dominated by reason. While the dictionaries previous to the eighteenth century had been concerned with 'words', the encyclopedic dictionaries put more importance on the 'things' designated by the words. Diderot (<u>Encyclopédie, ou dictionnaire raissoné des sciences et des arts,</u> 1751) is often considered the originator of this type of lexical activity.

With the appearance of historical linguistics toward the middle of the nineteenth century, we witness some modification in lexicographical methods. **Littré's** <u>Dictionnaire de la langue française</u> (originally, <u>Dictionnaire étymologique, historique et grammatical de la langue française</u>)

begun in 1846, and published between 1863 and 1872, was the
first to be animated by historical preoccupations (etymology,
orthographic variations, past usages, etc.). Actually, the
Littré is a dictionary of 'classical' French. It does not
go beyond the year 1820 for its selection of examples, most
of which are taken from an academic language. However, it
is different from previous dictionaries in its relative
freedom in the recording of morphological forms, in its
systematic use of quotations and examples, and in its concern for logic in the distinction and arrangement of meanings. At the end of the nineteenth century appeared the
<u>Dictionnaire général</u> of Darmesteter, Hatzfeld, and Thomas,
which made a significant contribution to French lexicography
(especially in its etymological coverage and in its deductive application of semantic rules).

The twentieth century is characterized by an increment in
dictionaries of all types, together with intensification in
lexicographical innovation. Significant types include <u>le
Dictionnaire alphabétique et analogique</u> of Paul Robert
(1953-64) which tried to reconcile the requirements of
modernity, history, logic, and objective description. Examples are chosen from contemporary literature as well as
classical literature. Expressions illustrating the usage of
the word also appear. Old lexical items are indicated by a
special symbol; different types of grammatical usage are
distinguished; and synonymic cross-references are numerous.
Of the smaller format, the <u>Dictionnaire encyclopédique pour
tous, Petit Larousse</u> (1966), <u>le Dictionnaire du français
contemporain</u> (1967), and more recently, the <u>Lexis</u> (1975) are
important. Finally, the <u>Trésor de la langue française:
dictionnaire de la langue du dix-neuvième et du vingtième
siècle</u> (4 vols. published to date), a **mammoth** enterprise
under the direction of Paul Imbs, which is computer-based,
should be mentioned. In a sense, it is an extension of the
original philosophy of the Littré, but more ambitious and
enthusiastic in scope: it claims to be national, international, convenient, and efficient. The reader is provided
information on word usage, acceptability, frequency, origin,
history, etc., to a maximum degree. One also finds individual articles dedicated to word-formation elements (prefixes and suffixes). One of the difficulties with such a
vast project is obviously that of drawing the limits to the
entries and definitions to be included.

3. The typological model that I am proposing utilizes
three primary classificatory criteria (or axes) and four
secondary ones. The former represent the most visible features of the dictionary and are called dictionary 'universal'
features. The latter refer more specifically to the structural content of the dictionary and represent 'genetic'

features. These are hierarchically ordered with respect to the former, which are situated along the same plane, so to speak. See Figure 1. The first type (I) classifies dictionaries on the basis of the number of languages involved; the second (II) classifies them according to the nature of the lexical units and their linguistic properties; and the third (III) classifies them according to the nature of the information or patterns of arrangement.

Under type I a dictionary may be classified as monolingual (or unilingual) involving only one language or multilingual (plurilingual) involving more than one language. Plurilingual dictionaries are said to be of the homoglossic type if they represent dialects of the same language (e.g. <u>Dictionnaire du patois forézien</u>, 1862), or if they represent different stages of the same language (<u>Dictionnaire d'ancien français</u>, 1880). They are said to be of the heteroglossic type if they represent two or more different language systems. If, for example, only two different language systems are considered (cf. Estienne's <u>Dictionnaire francais: latin</u>), the dictionary is bilingual heteroglossic; but if three or more languages are considered (e.g. <u>Dictiònnaire français, allemand, latin et allemand, français, Latin, 1610</u>), the dictionary is multilingual heteroglossic.

Under type II we distinguish linguistic (or language) dictionaries from encyclopedic dictionaries. If the nomenclature of the dictionary espouses all the lexical items of the language, the dictionary is considered linguistic (or language oriented) in type. If, on the other hand, the nomenclature includes additionally information about the extralinguistic world—physical or nonphysical—the dictionary is of the encyclopedic type. More specifically, the nomenclature of the encyclopedic dictionary is almost exclusively nominal, while that of the linguistic dictionary excludes proper nouns but otherwise represents the entire lexicon of a language. The encyclopedic dictionary has been considered as a double dictionary by some, since, on the one hand, it presents all the characteristics of a language dictionary, and on the other, all of the characteristics of an encyclopedia (i.e. description of the lexicon and description of the world). In Figure 1 language dictionaries (II-A) are further typed according to the extensive or restrictive nature of their nomenclature. They are considered specialized (II-A-2) if the nomenclature is somehow limited by restrictions that the lexicographer decides on a priori (e.g. <u>Dictionnaire d'argot</u>, <u>Dictionnaire de synonymes</u>, <u>Dictionnaire de linguistique</u>). The specialized dictionary represents a segment of the entire body of signs irrespective of their importance or relative frequency in the whole. General dictionaries (II-A-1) are different in that they are concerned with describing all of the nomenclature of the

Figure 1. Typology of French dictionaries.

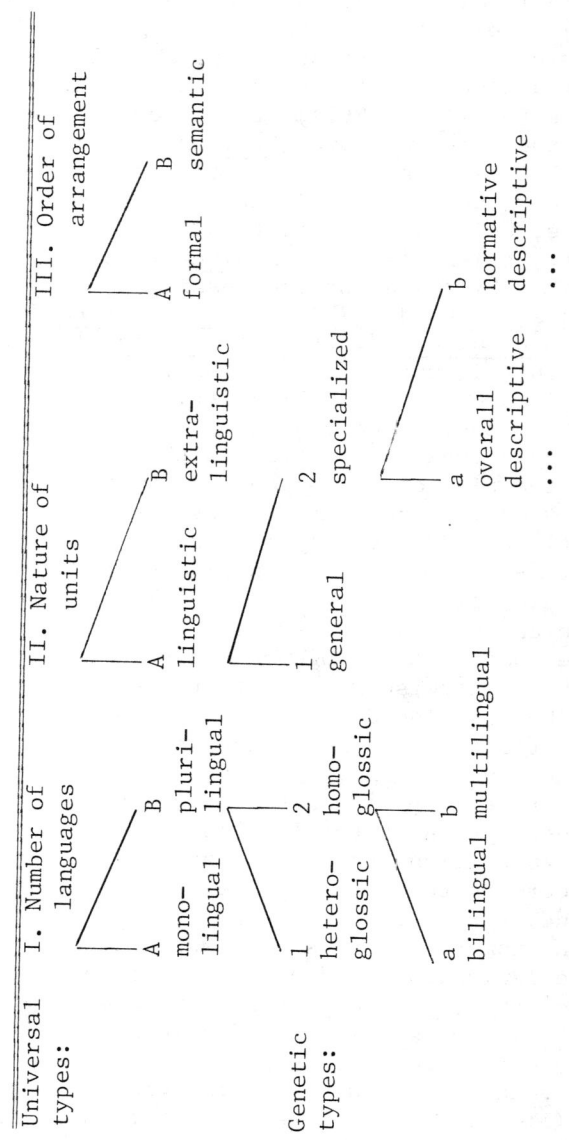

national language. If the particular focus of the general
type of dictionary is on regular usage in its so-called
purest form, the dictionary is considered normative descriptive (II--A-1-b). In such cases the lexicographer generally omits neologisms, archaisms, technical terms, and the
like. (See the previous comments about the <u>Dictionnaire de
l'Académie</u>.) In addition to the normative descriptive type
of general dictionary, one recognizes the overall descriptive type (II-A-1-a) which is more liberal in its selection
of lexical content. It describes much more than the standard
language used at the time of its compilation. For this type
of dictionary is also concerned with neologisms, rare words,
levels of language (popular speech, familiar speech, as well
as academic or normative speech), etc. The normative and
overall types of descriptive dictionaries demand further investigation. (We should expect additional **subtypes** to
emerge from such a detailed study.) However, I shall not
undertake this task at present. (See Zgusta 1971:209-212
for further information on the terms 'overall' and 'normative' descriptive.)

Under type III dictionaries are considered either formal
(III-A) if the arrangement of the lexical entries follows an
alphabetic or reverse alphabetic order, or semantic (III-B)
if the arrangement is of an analogical or conceptual order.

While the universal features (I, II, III) of the dictionary are easily identifiable, the genetic features are more
difficult to identify--they demand a closer examination of
the dictionary entries. The typology proposed here thus
forces us to make an initial choice (either I, II, or III--
but not necessarily in that chronological order). Once the
initial choice is made, we continue to choose types from the
intersecting categories. When a given dictionary does not
allow us to make a definitive 'either/or' choice, but rather
suggests that both choices are appropriate, we are forced
to recognize a heterogeneous or mixed type. Indeed, this is
no more uncommon in lexicographical activity than in the
field of dialectology, for example (cf. instances of dialect
mixture). Of course we always hope that our classifications
establish salient and significant features.

Given the criteria just mentioned, we are able to classify
Estienne's <u>Dictionnaire francois-latin</u>, Littré's <u>Dictionnaire
de la langue française</u> and Larousse's <u>Lexis</u> in the following
manner:

    Estienne: (I-B-1-a) + (II-A-1-b) + (III-A)
    Littré: (I-A) + (II-A-1-b) + (III-A)
    <u>Lexis</u>:   (I-A) + (II-A-1-a) + (III-A)

4. In this final section I shall comment upon the internal
structure of one dictionary in particular--the <u>Lexis</u>. The

Lexis (published in 1975 under the direction of Jean Dubois) is a monolingual linguistic dictionary of the overall descriptive general type. Its structure encompasses the most recent findings in the field of linguistics. Comprehensive articles are **subcategorized** according to criteria that are both semantic and morphological, thus allowing the reader to comprehend the processes that shape the French language. Current vocabulary is extensively treated. Grammatical terms (e.g. determinants, prepositions, conjunctions) are also a part of the stock, as are idioms and frozen expressions. Neologisms as well as classical items are treated, provided they cover a sufficiently large lexical field. A small place is also given to marginal words (e.g. dialect variants and regionalisms).

The order of arrangement is alphabetic, and the information on each article varies from a few lines to several columns. Different type faces are employed to distinguish various parts of the dictionary article. For example, the entry itself is in heavy **boldface** type. It is immediately followed by the standard pronunciation, transcribed phonetically according to IPA symbols, and the grammatical category of the word. Next comes a parenthesis which contains information of a historical nature (etymology and dating). Following this parenthesis, one finds a variety of information in square brackets, such as the conjugation of the verb, the plural of compound nouns, etc. Then comes the definition proper, preceded by an arabic number, if the word is polysemic. The definition is further specified by examples (set in italic type)--some fabricated by the editors; others, cited from literary sources, primarily from twentieth century authors. The example itself is further specified by synonyms and antonyms which are always accompanied by indications of the various levels of language and by notations of the intensity of the item. An arrow pointing upward (↑) indicates a synonym of stronger expressive value; one pointing downward (↓) **indi**cates a synonym of weaker expressive value.

Another original feature of the _Lexis_ is its attempt to present in each article a coherent semantic unit. Thus, it proceeds with two processes, closely complementing each other: the process of 'regrouping' (composing) and the process 'degrouping' (decomposing). Derivations and compounds are grouped together around a key word, to which their meanings are closely attached. The key word figures in the entry. The systems of suffixation (-_age_, -_ment_, -_eur_ (-_euse_), -_ation_, etc.) and of prefixation (_dé(s)_-, _ren_-, _re_- , etc.), allow the reader to reunite derivational series which are more or less complex. For example, starting from the adjective form _GRAND_, we derive, by the interplay of normal derivational processes, _GRANDEMENT_ (adv.), _grandet_, _grandelet_, _grandissisme_ (adjs.), _grandeur_ (nom.), _grandir_, _agrandir_ (verbes), etc.

These 'regroupings' allow us to understand the transformation of one word into another: verb into noun; adjective into noun; verb into another verb, etc.

The format of the Lexis also includes a dictionary of grammar (approximately 65 pages in length) which presents under alphabetic arrangement the rules (phonological, morphological, and syntactic) of the French language. Cross-references send the reader from the dictionary article to the dictionary of grammar when a concise explanation is needed. Figure 2 shows three sample entries from the Lexis. The first illustrates the special treatment of prefixes and suffixes, the second illustrates a typical 'popular' term, and the third illustrates a typical polysemic entry.

Figure 2. Three sample entries from Lexis.

MINI- préfixe, emprunté au Lat. MINI(MUM), servant à former des substantifs. Les composés sont traités à l'ordre du composant principal.

YÉ-YÉ [jeje] adj. et n. (d'un refrain de chanson yeah, alter. de yes; 1962). Fam. Se dit des chanteurs qui utilisent un rythme particulier venu des Etats-Unis, de leurs jeunes admirateurs, du style et du comportement des uns et des autres: La mode yé-yé. Il n'est pas très yé-yé.

DICTIONNAIRE [diksjɔnɛR] n.m. (lat. médiév. dictionarium, de dictio, -onis, locution, 1539). 1. Recueil des mots ou d'une catégorie de mots d'une langue, généralement rangés par ordre alphabétique (mais parfois classés par ordre de matières ou par analogies) et expliqués dans la même langue ou traduits dans une autre: Le Dictionnaire de l'Académie. Le dictionnaire étymologique donne l'origine des mots. Dictionnaire de langue. Avec le dictionnaire Larousse en sept volumes tu as Stanley Timour, Gustave-Adolphe et pas mal d'autres (Duhamel). Le dictionnaire bilingue donne la traduction des mots d'une langue dans une autre. 2. Ouvrage dans lequel on traite, par ordre alphabétique, les matières relatives à un objet quelconque, à une science, à un art ou, même, à toutes les connaissances humaines: Faut-il lui parler du dictionnaire de médecine? (Arland)// Dictionnaire encyclopédique, dictionnaire qui, outre les définitions de mots, contient des développements scientifiques, techniques, historiques, etc. 3. C'est un dictionnaire vivant, c'est une personne dont les connaissances sont fort étendues. ◆ dico n.m. (1885). Fam. Abrév. de DICTIONNAIRE.

5. Conclusion. I would like to close on a note of admiration and enthusiasm for an area of research that has made extraordinary progress in France over the last four and a half centuries. Although I have mentioned but a mere handful of the existing stock of dictionaries, you can surmise that the field of lexicography, which had its humble beginnings in France in the sixteenth century, with the appearance of Estieene's French-Latin bilingual dictionary, has come a long way. A proliferation of lexical activity has prompted linguists to study the structural differences and similarities in dictionaries and to attempt to establish theories about their classifications. The typology for French dictionaries which I have outlined makes such an attempt. This typology begins by defining the concept of dictionary (as opposed to other lexical activity), and then proceeds to identify universal and genetic dictionary features. It maintains simplicity and clarity throughout. One cannot justifiably speak in terms of a 'pure' type of dictionary any more than one can speak in terms of a 'pure' accent. But if a typology can not characterize 'pure' types, it can group dictionaries according to their most significant commonly shared properties and then make general comments about them. This is very useful information.

REFERENCES

Authors

Catach, Nina, Jeannette Golfand, Odette Mettas, Liselotte Pasques. 1976. Le Dictionnaire historique de l'orthographe française. Le Français Moderne 1.57-67.
Malkiel, Yakov. 1959. Distinctive features in lexicography: A typological approach to dictionaries exemplified with Spanish. Romance Philology 12.366-399; 13.111-155.
Malkiel, Yakov. 1960. A typological classification of dictionaries on the basis of distinctive features. In: Problems in lexicography. Edited by F. W. Householder and Sol Saporta. Bloomington: Indiana University, 1962. 3-24.
Matore, Georges. 1968. Histoire des dictionnaires français. Paris: Larousse.
Quemada, Bernard. 1968. Les dictionnaires du français moderne 1539-1863; Etude sur leur histoire, leurs types et leurs méthodes. Paris: Didier.
Rey, Alain. 1970. Typologie génétique des dictionnaires. Langages 19.48-68.
Rey-Debove, Josette. 1971. Etude linguistique et sémiotique des dictionnaires français contemporains. The Hague: Mouton.
Zgusta, Ladislav. 1971. Manual of lexicography. The Hague: Mouton.

Dictionaries

Dictionnaire francois-latin. By Robert Estienne. 1539.
Thresor de la Langue francoyse. By J. Nicot. 1606.
A dictionary of the French and English tongues. By Cotgrave. 1611.
Dictionnaire francois contenant les mots et les choses. By Richelet. 1680.
Dictionnaire universel. By Furetière. 1690.
Dictionnaire de l'Académie française, Anonymous. 1694.
Encyclopédie, ou dictionnaire raisonné des sciences et des arts. By Diderot and Alembert. 1751.
Dictionnaire de la langue française. By **Littré**. 1863.
Dictionnaire général de la langue française. By Darmesteter, Hatzfeld, et Thomas. 1920.
Dictionnaire alphabétique et analogique de la langue française, les mots et les associations d'idées. By P. Robert. 1964.
Dictionnaire encyclopédique pour tous. Petit Larousse. 1966.
Dictionnaire du français contemporain. By Dubois et al. 1967.
Trésor de la langue française; dictionnaire de la langue du XIXe et du XXe siècle, vol. I. 1971.
Lexis: Dictionnaire de la langue française. By Dubois. 1975.

DEGAPPING THE LEXICON OF SPANISH VERBS

JOHN J. STACZEK
Florida International University

As new lexical items continue to appear in the Spanish language, their appearance, at least historically, has been attributed to such intralanguage and interlanguage mechanisms as borrowing and analogy. On the morphological level it is not difficult to predict how and in what form new items will enter a language. In Spanish, for example, the effect can be achieved in the following way: a verb morpheme can be attached to an already existing nominal or adjectival root to produce such forms as <u>telexiar</u> 'send by telex' or <u>alfombrar</u> 'cover the floor with a carpet'. However, the processes whereby new lexical items are produced are far more complex than simple morphological change might indicate. Beyond the level of morphology, no attempts have been made to account for new verbal phenomena such as <u>aguacerear</u> 'storm, rain heavily', <u>amercurizar</u> 'land on Mercury', <u>emproblemar</u> 'cause problems' and the like. There are, however, as a result of the recent linguistic analyses of Charles Fillmore, Wallace Chafe, George Lakoff, and James McCawley, several semantically based devices which would explain the appearance of new verbs where voids or gaps in the lexicon have previously existed and may yet exist. The purpose of this paper is to explore these semantically based mechanisms to see where and how Spanish can begin to fill in its gaps.

Taken in order of ascending degree of abstraction, the mechanisms are: (1) a type of lexical incorporation as suggested by Fillmore (1971); (2) a version of the bidirectional derivation scheme as suggested by Chafe (1970) and Cook (1973, 1974); and (3) a version of the unidirectional semantic mechanism as suggested by Lakoff (1971) and McCawley (1968).

In his semantic description of lexical items (1971c) Fillmore alludes to the notion of lexical decomposition or its converse, lexical incorporation, namely, that

Certain kinds of lexical items can be used as predicates semantically but cannot themselves occur as surface predicate words. Such words will appear in the syntactic position expected of some other constituent ... and there must therefore be lexically associated with them some predicator word ... capable of bearing tense and aspect properties that can only be attached to verblike elements. The constituents ... are those of the type '<u>have</u> faith in', '<u>give</u> credence to', '<u>be</u> loyal to', etc., and the predicator words ... include <u>be</u>, <u>do</u>, <u>give</u>, <u>have</u>, <u>make</u>, <u>take</u>, and a few others. (Fillmore 1971c:389)

The suggestion here is that at the lexical level there seem to exist certain lexical primes such as <u>dar</u> 'give', <u>hacer</u> 'do, make' and <u>poner</u> 'put' (Staczek 1976) which, in combination with nominal objects and sometimes with locatives, will incorporate the objects or locatives thus producing a new lexical item which is morphologically related to the incorporated element. To illustrate, then, <u>dar</u> incorporates <u>beso</u> 'kiss' to produce <u>besar</u> 'to kiss', <u>golpe</u> to <u>golpear</u> 'beat', <u>ayuda</u> to <u>ayudar</u> 'help', <u>susto</u> 'scare' to <u>asustar</u> 'scare', etc. <u>Hacer</u> would do the same with <u>pregunta</u> 'question' to produce <u>preguntar</u> 'question', <u>dibujo</u> 'drawing' to <u>dibujar</u> 'draw', <u>viaje</u> 'trip' to <u>viajar</u> 'travel'; <u>poner</u> would incorporate <u>silla</u> 'chair, saddle' to produce <u>ensillar</u> 'saddle', <u>cubierta</u> 'cover' to produce <u>cubrir</u> 'cover' as suggested by Kirschner (1976). <u>Poner</u> also allows the incorporation of a locative such as <u>poner X en latas</u> 'in cans' to produce <u>enlatar</u> 'can' <u>en botellas</u> 'in bottles' to <u>embotellar</u> 'bottle', <u>en grupos</u> 'in groups' to <u>agrupar</u> 'group', etc. Examples of this type of lexical incorporation are numerous in Spanish and to a large degree meaning is preserved in the incorporation, as for example, in (1) and (2).

(1) Ana embotelló la gaseosa.
    'Ana bottled the soda.'
(2) Ana puso la gaseosa en botellas.
    'Ana put the soda in bottles.'

I purposely say 'to a large degree' because there are instances in which the meaning of a sentence in paraphrase can change, for example, (3) and (4), for which I am indebted to Kirschner (1976).

(3) Juan encoló la mesa.
    'Juan glued the table.'
(4) Juan puso la cola en la mesa.
    'Juan put the glue on the table.'

The incorporation process proceeds as in these examples
and has the potential for producing items such as favorecer
'hacer o dar un favor' in addition to its more frequent
interpretation as 'apoyar en su intento'; other items are

babear 'drool'	hacer babas 'make droolings'
emproblemar 'cause problems'	poner en problemas 'put into a problem situation'
engavetar 'put in a drawer'	poner en una gaveta 'put in a drawer'
americurizar 'put or land on Mercury'	poner en Mercurio 'put on Mercury'

The incorporation scheme just described appears to be limited
because of (1) already existing forms with a different semantic interpretation, hence an artificial incorporation, and
(2) a large number of borrowings from other languages of already incorporated forms.

The second type of semantic mechanism is the bidirectional
derivation scheme proposed by Chafe (1970) and modified by
Cook (1973, 1974) and Staczek (1973) in which Chafe suggests
that all verbs are specified in terms of three semantic or
selectional units, namely, state, process, and action which
account for four verb types, namely, state, process, action,
and action-process. It should be noted that Cook and Staczek
have shown that action predicators are no more than action-
process predicators that have coreferential agent and patient
roles. Consequently, a modification based on four derivational units that add or subtract roles from a predicator, is
introduced in the bidirectional mechanism to produce the
following configuration.

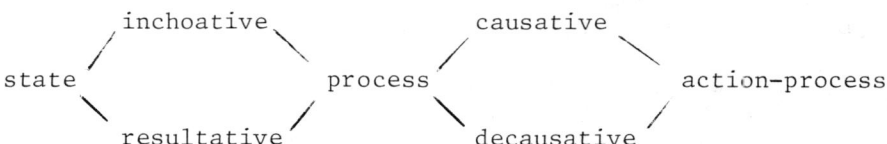

These derivational units allow the speaker, once a lexical
choice has been made, to convert, for example, 'a verb root
which is intrinsically a state into one that is derivatively
a process' (Chafe 1970:123).

The four derivational units permit the addition or sub-
traction of a feature or role in such a way as to convert,
for example, action-process verbs such as cortar 'cut', which
in (4) is a transitive verb,

(4) Juan cortó la tela.
    'Juan cut the material.'

to a <u>process</u> verb which in (5) is intransitive.

(5) La tela corta fácilmente.
   'The material cuts easily.'

Sentences (4) and (5) further illustrate that as the predicators are manipulated with respect to the noun roles which occur with them, certain syntactic changes also occur, namely, that from transitive to intransitive usage, as the Agent is deleted the direct object assumes the role of subject in a <u>process</u> verb. The process is completely reversible as the derivational scheme suggests; the Agent may be added to the <u>process</u> root to produce an <u>action-process</u> root; the inchoative derivation and its converse, resultative, as well as the causative derivation and its converse, decausative, provide for right to left derivation.
A more detailed account of the derivational procedure proposed by Chafe shows that the feature <u>inchoative</u> converts <u>state</u> verbs to <u>process</u> verbs, as in (6) and (7).

(6) Pablo está cansado.
   'Pablo is tired.'
(7) Pablo se cansa fácilmente.
   'Pablo gets tired easily.'

In (7), the subject is coreferential with another element, the reflexive <u>se</u>; this syntactic consequence is typical of a number of verbs which are inchoatively derived (Staczek 1973). The feature causative, when added to the already inchoatively derived root of (7) converts a <u>process</u> to an <u>action-process</u> as in (8),

(8) Pablo cansa a su mujer.
   'Pablo tires his wife.'

which three, taken together, show that noun roles are added to produce different verb types. The converse of both processes, namely, 'decausative' and 'resultative', respectively, will allow us to return to the <u>state</u> form of the predicator. In order to further illustrate the procedure, we might choose the Spanish verb <u>azular</u> 'give a blue tint to' or *'bluen' if there were no gap in English. Sentences (9)-(11) illustrate the point.

(9) El pintor azuló el cristal.
   'The painter gave a blue tint to the glass.'
(10) El cristal se azuló.
    'The glass became blue.'
(11) El cristal está azul.
    'The glass has a blue tint to it.'

Granted, if the verb in (9)-(11) had been related to blanco 'white', the examples might have been less 'rebuscados'. If Spanish, to take this several steps further, has forms like achicar 'shorten' or alargar 'lengthen', or enniñecer 'make child-like', the same processes can apply to forms such as *afear 'make ugly' as opposed to alindar 'make pretty', or *enfrescar or *frescar 'make cool, cool' as opposed to enfriar 'make cold' or calentar 'heat, warm', etc. It would seem that because the mechanism is clearly there already, the gaps, when the need arises, can begin to disappear.
It might be pointed out that in Chafe's derivational scheme it is possible to produce state forms of motion verbs; however, the notion of motion states is counterintuitive.

The third and final degapping mechanism is found at the deepest level of abstraction, the level at which linguists such as McCawley, Lakoff, and Binnick talk about abstract predicates or semantic primes. At this level, McCawley and Lakoff have developed (1968:197) a unidirectional semantic mechanism for deriving states into inchoatives into causatives, for example, in McCawley's analysis of the verb kill as cause to die, that is, that there is a structure provided at the deepest level which accounts for complex predicates as superordinate and subordinate trees as in Figure 1.

Figure 1.

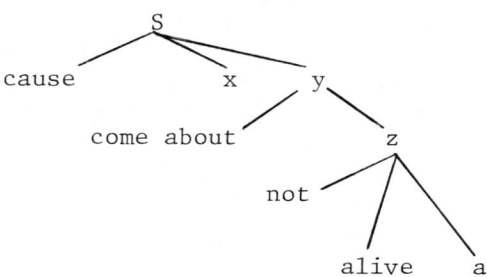

which produces something such as (12),

(12) Peter causes Paul to become not alive.

which in at least one sense could be interpreted as (13).

(13) Peter killed Paul.

For our purposes, not as a semantic prime will not be treated because it is more profitably pursued in generative semantics as operating at any level producing any number of different readings according to where it appears as a constituent. In this unidirectional mechanism, we find the highest predicate to be that of CAUSE with two arguments accompanying it, one of which will be an embedding of another complex predicate. At the second level, we find INCHOATIVE as a predicate with a single argument dominating another single argument predicate STATE. The path that is followed in the derivation is from STATE to INCHOATIVE to CAUSE under the assumption that at the lowest level in the derivation there must be a state predicate. Though similar to the bidirectional mechanism proposed by Chafe with respect to state, inchoative, and cause, the combined Lakoff-McCawley mechanism will proceed in a single direction--upward.

The upward motion of the derivation assumes that the lower level is somehow lexicalized into the higher tree producing a new and sometimes different predicate. This can be illustrated with triste 'sad', entristecerse 'become sad', and entristecer 'sadden', namely, state, inchoative, or process (intransitive) and causative or action-process (transitive).

Before attempting to illustrate some degapping I might reiterate that there is no stative form of a motion verb; hence, there is a semantic as well as lexical gap. The derivation, it would seem, would begin at an inchoative level. If it were possible to posit a motion state it could only be done within the context of temporal and spatial parameters, that is, at points t_1, t_2, t_n in a motion in which the state described differs from the previous state. This is only a speculation, one based on an analogy with a motion picture which on film describes motion at an infinite number of temporal and spatial points.

With motion states out of the way, we can proceed to some derivations following the upward movement in the mechanism. Azular 'give a blue tint to' enniñecer 'make child-like' and other verbs described earlier, would all derive from a stative base through a process of inclusion in a higher predicate. All verbs derived from states described by an adjective fit the same pattern and, based on morphological analogy, would produce new verbs such as *afear, *enfrescar, or frescar, for example.

The next two items are found in Miami-Cuban Spanish and seem to point to the derivation just described. Regresar 'return' (intransitive) is used transitively and appears to be embedded in a cause predicate at a higher level, as in (14), for example,

(14) Regresé al perro al garage.

'I $\begin{Bmatrix}\text{made}\\\text{caused}\end{Bmatrix}$ the dog to return to the garage.'

and (15).

(15) Llegaron el bulto a Chicago.
'They caused the package to be returned to Chicago.'

In both (14) and (15) there is a compression of the middle inchoative level and a higher causative level. Normally, in Spanish, these sentences would be complex with a matrix hacer or causar plus an embedded subjunctive. In any event the phenomena have been observed among educated speakers; I have chosen to interpret them as manifestations of the unidirectional derivational mechanism because they permit the lexicalization of an abstract predicate and add new meaning to verbs for which there has been a gap at the causative level.

Although only a handful of verbs has been shown to be derivable according to the three mechanisms described, I am certain that others can and will be derived as Spanish continues to evolve and fill in some of the lexical gaps. Beyond morphology, there exist at the semantic level mechanisms to support the degapping; at the lexical level, the gaps can be seen to diminish as the need for incorporated complex forms develops.

REFERENCES

Anderson, John M. 1971. The grammar of case: Towards a localistic theory. Cambridge: Cambridge University Press.
Binnick, Robert. 1968. On the nature of the lexical item. CLS 4.1-11. Chicago: Chicago Linguistic Society.
Chafe, Wallace. 1970. Meaning and the structure of language. Chicago: University of Chicago Press.
Cook, Walter A. 1974. Case grammar and generative semantics. In: Georgetown University Papers on Languages and Linguistics, Number 8. Washington, D.C.: Georgetown University Press.
Cook, Walter A. 1973. Covert case roles. In: Georgetown University Papers on Languages and Linguistics, Number 7. Washington, D.C.: Georgetown University Press.
Dowty, David R. 1972. Studies in the logic of verb aspect and time reference in English. Unpublished dissertation.
Fillmore, Charles J. 1971a. Verbs of judging: An exercise in semantic description. In: Studies in linguistic semantics. Edited by Charles J. Fillmore and D. Terence Langendoen. New York: Holt, Rinehart and Winston.
Fillmore, Charles J. 1971b. Some problems for case grammar. In: Georgetown University Round Table on Languages and Linguistics, 24. Edited by Richard J. O'Brien. Washington, D.C.: Georgetown University Press.
Fillmore, Charles J. 1971c. Types of lexical information. In: Semantics: An interdisciplinary reader. Edited by Danny Steinberg and Leon Jakobovits. Cambridge: Cambridge University Press.

Fillmore, Charles J. 1968. The case for case. In: Universals in linguistic theory. Edited by Emmon Bach and Robert T. Harms. New York: Holt, Rinehart and Winston.
Kirschner, Carl. 1976. Generative semantics and Spanish. Unpublished dissertation.
Lakoff, George. 1976. Towards generative semantics. In: Syntax and semantics 7: Notes from the linguistic underground. Edited by James D. McCawley. New York: Academic Press.
Lakoff, George. 1970. Irregularity in syntax. New York: Holt, Rinehart and Winston.
McCawley, James D., ed. 1976. Syntax and semantics 7: Notes from the linguistic underground. New York: Academic Press.
McCawley, James D. 1971. Prelexical syntax. In: Georgetown University Round Table on Languages and Linguistics, 24. Edited by Richard J. O'Brien. Washington, D.C.: Georgetown University Press.
McCawley, James D. 1968. Lexical insertion in a transformational grammar without deep structure. CLS 4.71-80. Chicago: Chicago Linguistic Society.
Staczek, John J. 1976. La descomposición léxica en español. In: Thesaurus 31. Bogotá: Instituto Caro y Cuervo.
Staczek, John J. 1973. Problems in case grammar arising from an analysis of Spanish text. Unpublished dissertation.
Wierzbicka, Anna. 1976. Mind and body. In: Syntax and semantics 7: Notes from the linguistic underground. Edited by James D. McCawley. New York: Academic Press.

CULTURAL VALUES
AND LEXICAL FEATURES IN SPANISH GRAMMAR

BRUCE G. STIEHM
University of Pittsburgh

I will attempt to demonstrate that some of the most difficult Spanish grammar questions are lexical or supralexical in nature, that their formulation requires entering semantic features at various points in the grammatical description, and that there exist suggestive parallels between the more relativistic of these semantic features and corresponding principal values encountered in Spanish culture.
 I will argue that these relationships support a linguistic model in which: (1) semantic forces function at all points to constrain the grammatical calculus, and (2) cultural structure influences linguistic structure through lexical and supralexical form-meaning correspondences. The first of these assertions is in harmony with generative semantic precepts. The second is not a rewarming of the Whorf-Sapir hypothesis but rather incorporates the coordinate operation of relativist and universal determinants of structure in culture, the lexicon, and grammar.
 I will summarize and comment upon six Spanish grammar questions: the prepositions, the preterit-imperfect, *ser-estar*, the subjunctive vs. the indicative, fixed word order, and free word order. Since none of these questions has been definitively settled, I will strive to reflect this unsettledness in my discussion.

Prepositions. María Luisa López (1970) underlines in her extensive study the varying semantic and syntactic nature of the preposition. For example, *de* may be full of meaning as in *viene del lago*, or it may be a relatively empty element in which the syntactic function predominates, as in *un hombre* de seís pies, or de hacerlo así. The preposition a has similar possibilities. It is full of meaning in voy a Sevilla, but is predominantly syntactic in le miré a María, or llovió a cántaros.

But, as María Luisa López demonstrates, there is no simple division between when a preposition is semantically full and when it is relatively empty. There is, rather, on the abstract level of rules and competence, a well-defined semantic feature connected with each preposition. It is a feature of relation that is in opposition to the contrasting relational features connected with the other prepositions. At the level of performance, however, when a preposition is placed in context, the connected feature may be intensified or attenuated by the preposition's greater or lesser semantic or syntactic role (López 1970:145-155). In any case, the underlying semantic feature is the same, and the syntactic function of the preposition usually bears an analogy to the lexical meaning conveyed in other contexts. None of this, of course, obviates the frequent neutralization of contrasts between prepositions, as in dar a beber vs. dar be beber, or daba vueltas en torno de la mesa vs. daba vueltas en torno a la mesa (López 1970:158-159).

As Pottier and others remarked before María Luisa López, the relationships expressed by the prepositions derive from universal spatial relations, which are also reflected in temporal and notional analogs. Moreover, in the context of philosophy of language, Uhlan von Slagle (1974) has attested that the spatial relations expressed by prepositions in many languages are semantic universals inherent to human thought and are expressed somehow by all languages, though not necessarily through prepositions. This semantic universality will affect the shape of the linguistic model.

What is significant in the foregoing for purposes of my discussion is: (1) the prepositions connect well-defined semantic features with a lexical form, (2) the connected feature also underlies most of the preposition's syntactic functions (this must be interpreted as the lexical entry of a semantic feature which exercises a syntactic constraint), and (3) the features connected with the prepositions are by the accounts of many philosophers and psychologists universal to human thought and perception.

Preterit-imperfect. William E. Bull (1960, 1965) applied his formulation of aspect to the description of the Spanish preterit and imperfect. In his well-known explanations, Bull asserted that aspect involves two ways of viewing events. Imperfective aspect (attached to the imperfect form) is associated with an event viewed as ongoing. Perfective aspect (attached to the preterit form) is associated with an event that is viewed as begun or ended.

Bull also pointed out that the two aspects combine with different features of context to develop the various meanings used in textbooks to explain the preterit-imperfect. Typical of these contexts are adverbs and cyclic vs. noncyclic events, which are so well known they need no exemplification.

Important to my discussion is: that the preterit and imperfect forms attach directly to semantic features that point to attitudinal referents in private experience. They are thus lexical in nature, and the occurrence of the semantic feature constrains an obligatory grammatical choice. Contrasted to the prepositions, however, the perfective-imperfective opposition is crystallized in Spanish in a uniquely Hispanic manner, and therefore reflects the relativist aspects of the culture.

Ser-estar. Mercedes Roldán (1974a,b) adds a remarkably elegant contribution to the formulation of ser-estar. Her semantic-based analysis states simply that both verbs are copula possessing distinct semantic features. The feature attached to ser is 'existence', while estar presupposes 'existence' and additionally bears the feature 'permanence at locus'. Existence incorporates not just the fact of something existing, but also its existing as a predicate of another element. The features explained previously by Bull as effects of ser-estar (e.g. 'change' vs. 'no change', with adjectives, or 'active' vs. 'stative' with past participles) are shown to result from the transfer of semantic features in other elements. The same rationale is convincingly applied to the ser passive, the estar progressive, and other constructions.

The most important insights here are that once again we are dealing with semantic features attached to lexical forms that point to attitudinal referents held in private experience. Moreover, the semantic feature again constrains an obligatory syntactic choice. Like the preterit-imperfect, ser-estar are crystallized in the language in a uniquely Hispanic way.

Subjunctive vs. indicative. Uniquely Hispanic too is the Spanish subjunctive. But who can summarize the subjunctive? Bolinger (1974, 1976) and Lozano (1972, 1975) have gone back and forth on it for a few years. Part of its great interest is how it overflows the formalizing bounds of linguistic theory.

The dialog between Bolinger and Lozano has clarified that it is not enough to define the semantic features contained in the expressions governing the subordinate clause, although such definition is useful. Like the preterit-imperfect and ser-estar, the subjunctive-indicative contrast is cued by semantic features that point to private attitudes concerning the content of the subordinate clause. Those attitudes can be summarized rigorously as 'factive' for the indicative and 'nonfactive' for the subjunctive. But a satisfactory description should probably specify that nonfactive includes such traditional categories as will, emotion, indefiniteness, unreality, unrealized future, etc. (see Bolinger 1974:466). It would also say that the governing expression is usually compatible with those attitudes (e.g. <u>dudo que sea así</u>), but that the attitude feature may often override the governing expression in some environments (e.g. <u>dudo que es así</u>), and that it is often the only determinant in others (<u>supongo que vayas a ir</u>).

An additional qualification that must be made is that the subjunctive's attitudinal feature is not connected in a lexical fashion with the verb form. It is instead associated with the verb plus the rest of the subordinate clause, and it colors the interpretation of the governing expression. It is attached to a complex lexico-syntactic configuration. The attitudinal feature is lexical, in that it adds referential meaning to the configuration, but it does so in the same way that intonation adds its distinguishing force to phonetic segments, by spanning a group. For this reason, I choose to strike a terminological parallel and refer to the attitudinal feature of the Spanish subjunctive as being supralexical.

Notice that once again we have in Spanish a private semantic feature exercising an obligatory syntactic constraint. However, now the point of entry is not through a single lexical element, but through a lexico-syntactic configuration. In a generative formulation, it would have to be entered via a transformation, after the basic phrase marker had been syntactically and lexically defined.

Fixed word order. Fixed word order in Spanish **nonsentence** constructions conforms to an archetypal sequence that places privative elements first (<u>no</u>, <u>todo</u>), followed by deictics (determiners, conjunctive pronouns), functional elements (auxiliary verbs, adverbs in <u>-mente</u>), quantifiers (numerals, limiting adjectives, quantitative adverbs), and lexical qualifiers (descriptive adjectives, adverbs).

Here again we are dealing with a lexico-syntactic configuration, constrained now by a feature of well-formedness, possibly both semantic and syntactic. But where would this constraint apply? In phrase structure? In surface structure? This is an open question. Since various other languages demonstrate similar fixed order, this structure must be considered quasi-universal. It also appears to be **supralexical**.

Free word order. Heles Contreras (1976) has treated Spanish free word order in depth, adding to the insights of Bolinger, Hatcher, and Praguean authors. Following their lead, he has constructed a set of transformational rules constrained by rhemic semantic features. Stress assignment is included, to account for tradeoffs between stress and some free order.

In brief, the rules apply a rheme selection hierarchy based on case grammar categories to determine which element belongs nearer to the end of the sentence.

We must again question where to enter these rules and their associated semantic constraints. Their transformational nature may place them in the transformational component; but the assignment of stress must place them nearer to surface structure, and perhaps very close to the phonological rules. Like the subjunctive and fixed order, the rhemic feature is supralexical. And like fixed order, the rhemic values appear attached to free order in many languages, and are perhaps quasi-universal.

The Spanish grammar questions I have summarized attach a semantic feature to a lexical or supralexical form. In all cases but the prepositions, the semantic features point to attitudinal referents held in private experience. In the prepositions, too, there is a notional analog of spatial relation underlying most syntactic uses. Finally, all of these questions incorporate semantic features constraining obligatory grammatical choices.

It is of interest to the consideration of the linguistic model that these features associate with lexical and supralexical forms, and that they appear to be entered at various points in the model. It is of great interest to the consideration of the relation between language and culture that Spanish has crystallized within it this collection of grammatical choices that center on communicating private attitudes. The combined effect is one of intensified attention to inner thoughts and feelings, to the definition of the boundaries between inner experience and the outer world, and to a formalized effort at making connections between the inner lives of persons and between those inner lives and the outer world. To refer to the cultural correlates of these aspects of Spanish, I will use the metaphors 'the garden', 'the wall', and 'the sword'. I can discuss them only quite briefly.

In the garden, Spanish culture cultivates the inner life, one's own and in intimacy with others. This concentration on inwardness, the ego, and intimacy is reflected in aspects of the subjunctive (will, emotion) and free order (theme-rheme focuses on communicating the unknown to another person). In social organization these Hispanic values are realized through the centrality of individuals and the family, the tertulia, the paseo, the **dedication** to leisure, the pervasiveness of religion. In literature, there are myriad examples of an intense concern with inwardness and intimacy--in the twentieth century, for example, Antonio Machado, Juan Ramón Jiménez, Pedro Salinas, García Lorca.

The wall surrounds the Spanish garden, and the Spanish house has its outer doors and windows barred. There is an attempt to set and defend definite boundaries between the inner life and the outer world. This may be seen reflected in the distinctions between the preterit (past action in a concrete context) and imperfect (past action bearing only its conceptual content), <u>ser</u> (the reduction to existential and conceptual essence) and <u>estar</u> (existence plus an enduring concrete locus), subjunctive (indefiniteness, unreality) and indicative (definiteness, reality). In Spanish society, these values are realized in the barriers set between the family and strangers, between one's community and other communities, between the nation and other nations. To these values can partially be ascribed the peculiarly Hispanic rhythm of monolithic conservatism alternating with explosive change. In literature, the topic of inner life relating to the outer world is a major theme that extends from earliest authors through the <u>Quijote</u>, Calderón (<u>La vida es sueño</u>) and Unamuno (<u>Niebla</u>) to present-day currents (Borges, García Márquez, Cortázar, etc.).

The sword is wielded against both the inner life and the outer world. I refer here to Hispanic voluntarism, in which both inner and outer reality are molded to fit the will. This creates the paradox that inner reality is treated as plastic and concrete, and the outer world as a malleable extension of inner concepts. These values are reflected principally in the subjunctive (emotion, will). In Spanish society, they are realized through intransigence in conflict, strong concepts of honor and pride, and heroic collective projects. In literature, this is also a principal theme which embraces Santa Teresa's striving for mystical union with God, Don Quijote's attempts to create an ideal order on earth, and Don Juan's idolatry of the will above all other natural or supernatural values and forces.

Turning to the linguistic model, let me introduce one last metaphor. Instead of conceiving of a linear connection between meaning and sound, in which syntax mediates absolutely, I believe we are better advised to think in terms of encapsulating layers by which culture surrounds meaning and meaning grammar, like the shell and white of an egg surround the yolk. Meaning, however, should also be seen as pervading the whole structure, constraining in many ways the grammatical and phonetic forms. With a model of this sort, I think we can proceed better to understand linguistic structure.

REFERENCES

Bolinger, Dwight L. 1974. One subjunctive or two? Hispania 57.462-471.
Bolinger, Dwight L. 1976. Again--one or two subjunctives? Hispania 59.41-49.
Bull, William E. 1965. Spanish for teachers. New York: Ronald Press.
Contreras, Heles. 1976. A theory of word order with special reference to Spanish. New York: North-Holland Publishing Co.
López, María Luisa. 1970. Problemas y métodos en el análisis de preposiciones. Madrid: Gredos.
Lozano, Anthony G. 1972. Subjunctives, transformations, and features in Spanish. Hispania 55.76-90.
Lozano, Anthony G. 1975. In defense of two subjunctives. Hispania 58.277-283.
Roldán, Mercedes. 1974a. Toward a semantic characterization of 'ser' and 'estar'. Hispania 57.68-75.
Roldán, Mercedes. 1974b. On the so-called auxiliaries 'ser' and 'estar'. Hispania 57.292-295.
Slagle, Uhlan von. 1974. Language, thought, and perception: A proposed theory of meaning. The Hague: Mouton (Janua Linguarum, Series Major, 98).

LEXICALIZATION OF
THE IRREGULAR PAST PARTICIPLE
IN HISPANO-ROMANCE UP TO
AND INCLUDING THE ALFONSINE PERIOD

SONIA RAMÍREZ WOHLMUTH
Roosevelt University

A study of the Latin perfect passive participle (p.p.p.) and its treatment in Hispano-Romance entails many complex problems such as the degree to which the eventual regularization and reduction of the Latin p.p.p. into two morphemic shapes in Hispano-Romance, namely /stem+ado/ and /stem+ido/, is dependent upon the arrangement and reduction of the four conjugations of Classical Latin (Cl. Latin) into three in Hispano-Romance; the perception as 'irregular' of those Latin participles which are morphophonemically complex and the ability of such forms to survive as participles despite their 'irregularity' (a concomitant of this problem is the relexicalization with other grammatical functions of those 'irregular' participles which do remain in the language but not as part of the verb paradigm); and the repartition of the grammatical functions of the p.p.p. in Cl. Latin and the continuation or alteration of these functions in Hispano-Romance.

The composition and morphology of the four conjugations of Cl. Latin provide valuable insights. The question at hand is to seek an explanation for the apparent strength of verb conjugations I (-ĀRE) and IV (-ĪRE) (to a lesser degree) against the weakness of conjugations II (-ĒRE) and III (-ĔRE). Among the various approaches available to the researcher is a quasi-statistical one in which conjugational strength may be established on the basis of sheer numerical predominance of the verbs in one or another conjugation. Ernout (1920:94-107) has obligingly furnished his readers with a partial verb count (the IVth conjugation is omitted from the verb census). The numbers in Figure 1 reveal the patent and indisputable numerical superiority of the Ist conjugation.

Figure 1.

Conjugation	Total number of verbs	Simple verbs
I	3620	1800
II	570	160
III	2400	570

Since the total number of verbs in each conjugation includes compounds, it is apparent that the IInd and IIIrd conjugations rely heavily upon these prefixed forms to achieve a disproportionately large total when compared to the number of simple verbs in the conjugation.

Quick reflection on the validity of the statistical approach prevented the undertaking of a time-consuming search for more reliable figures. Implied in the impressively large count of the Ist conjugation lies the key to a more meaningful approach. How is it that the Ist conjugation became so numerically dominant (perhaps at the expense of the other conjugations)? An answer to this question involves the concepts of productivity and paradigmatic regularity. What is really significant is not so much the number of verbs in any given conjugation but its ability to create new forms; and this ability is to a large degree contingent upon the simplicity and predictability of the paradigm. Those conjugations, then, which are both regular and homogeneous are better suited for survival.

Here, a textual footnote concerning primary and secondary verbs is pertinent. There existed in Latin a class of verbs formed by affixing the verb endings directly to the inherited Indo-European (IE) root. These were the primary verbs. Of course, the ability to create new primary verbs was lost as the language moved from one historical phase to another. Hence, the existence of secondary verbs, especially of a productive type, was of utmost importance if the verb conjugation was to thrive. Kuryłowicz (1964:105) analyzes the verb creation cycle in this fashion.

> The formations serving to renew the present system of course go back to different periods. The most recent type is represented by -i̯e/i̯o- derivatives, forming the base of the productive conjugations of the historical period: -ei̯e/o- (Lat. -ēre ...); -ai̯e/o- (Lat. -āre ...), etc. All these types are by their origin clearly denominal, secondarily only deverbative. The cycle of this semantic development is approximately the following:

primary → deverbative → denominal → deverbative
verb   noun   verb   verb

It is the phase to the right in the cycle which is of concern here, as well as the possibility of a complete closure of the cycle as opposed to a linear development, i.e. do certain inherited Latin verbs then become primary types for Hispano-Romance followed by new derivations of a productive nature?

I. -ARE. The composition of each conjugation may now be profitably examined beginning with the Ist. The Ist conjugation contained both primary and secondary verbs, the latter being denominal, deadjectival and deverbative. The primary verbs were of two types: monosyllabic (with full vowel grade) and disyllabic (with reduced vowel grade apparent in the perfect and p.p.p., e.g. DOMĀRE but DOMUĪ and DOMĬTUS. Regularization of these forms was inevitable. With the exception of STŌ, STĀRE (with strong perfect STETĪ, reflected in occasional Old Spanish estide), the other monosyllabics (ending in stressed ā) conformed to the predominant pattern of the Ist conjugation. Likewise, a unique verb DŌ, DĂRE was reinterpreted as *DĀRE.

As for the secondary verbs, many were derived from processes which continued to be productive, to the extent of absorbing derivative processes originally associated with other conjugations. Denominal verbs were numerous and although normally derived from the first declension, all declensions were evident in one or another form. (See examples in Figure 2.)

Figure 2.

1st decl.	corōna 'crown'	coronāre 'to crown'
2nd decl.	regnum 'kingdom, reign'	regnāre 'to rule, reign'
3rd decl.	laus, laudis 'praise'	laudāre 'to praise'
4th decl.	gustus, -ūs 'taste'	gustāre 'to taste'
5th decl.	glaciēs, -iēs 'ice'	glaciāre 'to freeze'

In addition, the causative suffixes -ĬGŌ (<AGŌ) and -FĬCŌ (<FACIŌ) departed from the conjugation class of the original verb, thus forming new, regular Ist conjugation denominal (and occasionally deadjectival) verbs, e.g. NAVIGĀRE 'to sail' (NAVIS+AGERE) and GLORIFICĀRE 'to glorify' (GLORIA+FACERE).

Deadjectival verbs initially formed a relatively small class but as the Ist conjugation became increasingly numerous, it attracted third declension adjectives which had

traditionally been part of deadjectival formations in other
conjugations. Thus, alongside original forms of the type
CAECĀRE 'to blind' (build on -US, -A, -UM type adjectives,
in this case CAECUS 'blind'), one finds verbs like *MOLLIARE
(>Sp. mojar; cf. MOLLĪRE 'to soften' <MOLLIS 'soft') which
according to Elcock (1960:115) resulted in a reinterpreta-
tion of the verb suffix so that a new, highly productive
suffix -IARE was abstracted (it was also extended to the
formation of denominal verbs).
   The productiveness of the deverbatives was much enhanced
by the existence of a large number of suffixes which were
attracted to the Ist conjugation.[1] The implication of these
suffixes is readily apparent for as Ernout remarks in 'Elimination des formes anomales', an article in <u>Probleme der
lateinischen Grammatik</u> (1973:226), the motivating force behind lexical changes or substitutions in Latin was its increasing predilection for paradigms characterized by simplicity and regularity. Thus many verbs of the IIIrd conjugation (occasionally IInd and IVth) gave way to intensive-
iterative forms in -TĀRE (also -SĀRE and -ITĀRE). This
practice did not exempt verbs within the Ist conjugation itself when they were irregular, so DOMITŌ is derived from
DOMŌ and CREPITŌ from CREPŌ. When both forms remain in the
language they are distinguished semantically. However, in
the case of NĀRE vs. NATĀRE 'to swim', only the latter passed
into Romance. Let it be reiterated that when the anomalous
primary verb survived the Darwinian process of elimination
in Vulgar Latin, it was necessarily regularized. Thus Sp.
quebrar (<CREPĀRE 'to crackle') shows no signs of the reduced vowel grade in the perfect CREPŬĪ and the perfect
participle CREPĬTUS; rather one finds remade, regularized
forms: quebré and quebrado.

   II. -ĒRE. The second conjugation as indicated by the verb
count given by Ernout had an inherent disadvantage. Furthermore, the strength of the conjugation was doubly weakened by
internal fragmentation regarding the origin of the verbs and
their consequent paradigmatic patterning. A very small group
of primary verbs with root in <u>-ē-</u> such as FLĒRE 'to weep'
were quickly eliminated in the popular language through the
increasingly frequent use of more regular synonyms. The
failure to thrive of verbs such as FLĒRE, NĒRE was due in
part to a uniqueness of form--a p.p.p in -ĒTUS as well as a
perfect in -Ē-VĪ in contrast to the typical forms of the
conjugation, participle in -ĪTUS corresponding to a perfect
in -UĪ. Although perhaps a fanciful explanation, it appears
that a mere lack of phonetic substance (the root was monosyllabic as well as a number of inflected forms) contributed
to the inability of these root verbs to compete. However,
primary verbs with a <u>TeT</u> root extended by <u>-ē-</u> continued

in Hispano-Romance, especially high frequency verbs such as HABĒRE, VIDĒRE.

The secondary verbs of the IInd conjugation were deverbative or deadjectival. Among the deverbatives were the stative verbs (formed with the root extended in -ē- and the -ye/o suffix). When these verbs had corresponding active forms, usually in the IIIrd conjugation, the confusion and eventual merger of the two was inevitable. Neither the subtle semantic distinction between verbs such as JACEŌ and JACIŌ nor their phonological differences, which grew increasingly difficult to perceive, could preserve the identity of the two. A second deverbative type made with the thematic -eye/-eyo failed to distinguish itself either semantically or morphologically, except through the presence of a related verb in the language. (These deverbatives usually had causative meaning and occasionally intensive-iterative meaning.) In general, if these verbs entered Hispano-Romance it was through a remaking, at times based on the p.p.p. The scheme in Figure 3 shows the semantic-morphological development.

Figure 3.

---

*SPENDŌ ⟶ SPONDEŌ (SPONSUS, p.p.p.) ⟶ *SPONSO (SPONSARE)
'I promise'   'I pledge (myself)',   ↓
   ↑   'I betroth'
Gr. σπενδω   Sp. esposar
                                            'to wed' (reciprocal and active)

The last group of secondary verbs in this conjugation is one which could have been expected to flourish yet did not, the deadjectival verbs.[2] The unexpected lack of productivity of the deadjectival formation (adjective stem + -ē- + ye/o) may be explained by two sources of competition: first, the extended deadjectival formation of the Ist conjugation with the new suffix -IARE, and second, the loss of the semantic distinction between deadjectivals such as RUBĒRE 'to be red', 'to blush', and RUBESCĒRE 'to become red', 'to blush'. The distinction between the stative connotation of the former and the inceptive connotation of the latter having been lost, the inchoative suffix -ESCĔRE became the productive suffix to which the abundant Hispano-Romance forms in -ecer bear witness.

III. ´-ĔRE. Although numerous, the IIIrd conjugation suffered from several highly detrimental weaknesses. First, there was the high degree of diversification within the conjugation: primary root verbs, primary verbs in -ye/o, and primary root verbs in which the present stem was modified.³ Secondary verbs consisted of two basic types, deadjectivals with inchoative -sk- and denominatives to -ŭ- stems.

Concerning the vitality of the different types, Ernout (1920:94-95) states that the root verbs constituted a significant portion of the simple verbs in the IIIrd conjugation. Since this set included some of the most frequent verbs in the language, by force of repetition the idiosyncratic forms survived. Thus DĪCERE, DŪCERE, TRAHERE and their compounds all entered Hispano-Romance despite evident paradigmatic irregularities in the perfect and the p.p.p. The second set of primary verbs (in -ye/o) which had been transferred from the IVth conjugation is also evident in Hispano-Romance, e.g. CAPIŌ, CAPĔRE > caber and SAPIŌ, SAPĔRE > saber

Of the secondary verbs, only the deadjectival with inchoative suffix became a productive type in Hispano-Romance (with or without accompanying prefix). Although the emergence of the suffix -ĔSCERE as a productive suffix did much to increase the population of the IIIrd conjugation, it did little to strengthen its paradigm (through regularization) and was perhaps detrimental through identification with the deadjectival formation of the IInd conjugation verbs.

The denominatives in -u- seemed to lend paradigmatic strength to the conjugation through the formation of the p.p.p. (although this was apparently only a passing phase). These secondary verbs were formed with nouns in -u- from the fourth declension, and the p.p.p. ended in -ŪTUS, a parallel to the long, stressed vowels in the Ist and IVth conjugations which had participles in -ĀTUS and -ĪTUS, thus STATŪTUS alongside AMĀTUS and AUDĪTUS. (Some root verbs also had a p.p.p. in -ŪTUS, e.g. VOLVŌ, originally VOLUŌ:VOLŪTUS.)

IV. ĪRE. The IVth conjugation like the others contained both primary and secondary verbs. Morphological differences between the two are not apparent since the primary verbs had roots extended by -ī- and the denominals and deadjectivals were formed from i-stem nouns and adjectives (with a few exceptions, e.g. CUSTODĪRE:CUSTOS and SERVĪRE:SERVUS). The loss of part of the primary verbs to the IIIrd conjugation was not significant as it affected a small number of verbs, only those with short radical syllables as these fulfilled the conditions for iambic shortening (the first step in the change of ī to ĕ; the second was the lowering of ĭ before r).

If not a populous class (although an exact count has not been furnished), the IVth conjugation did possess several strengths. The existence of a large group of denominal-deadjectival verbs was certainly an asset although this group was encroached upon by the highly productive Ist conjugation suffix in -IĀRE and the IIIrd conjugation suffix in -ĔSCĔRE. However, the true strength of this conjugation seems to lie in its morphological parallel to the Ist conjugation, the main difference being the characteristic vowel of the conjugation—ā for the Ist and ī for the IVth. Thus, alongside AM-Ā-VĪ, the IVth conjugation had AUD-Ī-VĪ (although this was not the only perfect formation of the IVth conjugation, nor perhaps even the predominant one), and in the p.p.p. AUD-Ī-TUS to Ist conjugation AM-Ā-TUS. With the exception of the diversity in the formation of the perfect tense (vowel lengthening, s-perfect or sigmatic perfect, and the perfect in -Ī-VĪ), the IVth conjugation presented few disadvantages in terms of paradigmatic irregularities.

An examination of the forms of the p.p.p. in light of regularity of inflection should further reveal the inherent weaknesses of conjugations II and III, thus providing motives for a merger of the two (with occasional IIIrd conjugation verbs being transferred to the IVth). The formative suffix of the Latin p.p.p. is the IE adjectival suffix *-to which had multiple uses in Latin.[4] This suffix was attached to the weak grade of the verb root since it carried the stress. The morphophonemic alternate in -so was the result of a type of epenthesis followed by assimilation, required when the verb root ended in a dental consonant, although occasional nonetymological -so is found through interference from the sigmatic perfect. Other phonetic readjustments such as voice assimilation also took place across the morpheme boundary. It is clear, then, that those verbs which had a stem extended by a long vowel (which naturally carried the stress) held a definite advantage over verbs where the suffix was attached directly to the verb root. Where the -to suffix, unaltered by assimilation was clearly visible, preceded by contrasting long vowels (especially -ā- and -ī-), it provided a convenient marker of conjugational distinction. (The would-be parallel forms in -ĒTUS, conjugation II, and -ŪTUS, conjugation III, failed to thrive.) In addition, the long vowels were present in other forms of the verb paradigm, again with their full value and carrying the stress, e.g. in the infinitive -ĀRE, -ĪRE (cf. -ĒRE but not ´-ĔRE) and in the *-w- perfect: -ĀVĪ, -ĪVĪ (cf. -ĒVĪ for root verbs such as PLEŌ, PLĒRE, PLĒVĪ).

By the Vulgar Latin period, then, the participles in -ĀTUS and -ĪTUS traditionally referred to as weak (because of desinence stress) proved to be the contrary. Participles in -ĬTUS (which corresponded largely to -ŬĪ perfects of the IInd and IIIrd conjugations) were subject to syncope if they had not already undergone the process historically, cf. SECŌ, SECŬĪ, SECTUS and V.L. *POSTO (<PONŌ, POSUĪ, POSĬTUS) > Sp. puesto. The treatment of these consonant clusters, both primary and secondary, often had the result of further removing them from the regular verb paradigm, where the suffix -Vdo (for Hispano-Romance) constituted an easily recognizable morphological shape. Examples of those irregular participles in Hispano-Romance where the difficulty of extracting a common suffix is apparent are the following: dicho, hecho, -cocho, frito, muerto, puesto, etc. It is unlikely that the native speaker could develop a feeling for (V)-cho and (C)-to, as well as occasional (V)-so, e.g. impreso, as morphophonemic alternates of -Vdo.

The simplicity and symmetry of the suffixes -ĀTUS and -ĪTUS led to their being identified as the forms which regularly corresponded to conjugations I and IV. What, then, were the forms corresponding to conjugations II and III? It would seem that these conjugations could only be designated the conjugations of the irregular p.p.p. This was clearly not a satisfactory arrangement for it went contrary to the principle of paradigmatic regularity. Thus the p.p.p. of the IInd and IIIrd conjugations was remade on the model of the IVth. Lausberg (1966:359) offers this explanation of the regularization:

> Obsérvese que es muy posible que la formación vendĭtus, al la 3ª conjugación (vendĕre) a la segunda (vendēre), se transformase en vendītus en esp. y port.: como -ĕ- pasa a -ē-, así -ĭ- se convierte en -ī-. En ese caso, el paso de la 3ª conjugación a la 2ª se habría realizado en esp. y port. en una época en que la ĭ latina todavía no había pasado a e̥.

An alternative explanation lies in the remaking of the perfect of 'regular' IInd and IIIrd conjugation verbs, i.e. those characterized by -ŬĪ in the perfect. These verbs were changed in the perfect from strong to weak, i.e. from stem stress (´-ŬĪ) to desinence stress (-ĪVĪ). Presumably the shift in accent could then have been transferred to the participle. Since there existed no precedent for a vocalism in -ē- (p.p.p.'s like PLĒTUS had been lost), the IVth conjugation model was copied in toto for the perfect.

Returning with new evidence (the p.p.p. formation) to the merger of the IInd and IIIrd conjugations, one now sees the following related weaknesses inherent in the paradigm (of conjugation III, especially). To begin, a parallel to long vowel + suffix which seems to define the Ist and IVth conjugations, is totally lacking in the other two conjugations. (See Figure 4.) Of the two conjugations, the IIIrd has the greater disadvantage because of the stem stressed infinitive which sets it apart as a distinctive class (one which survives in Gallo-Romance and Catalan, but not in Hispano-Romance). It is probable, that a general repugnance to

Figure 4.

Infinitive	Present-1st pl.	Pres. Perf.-1st pl.	p.p.p
amāre	amāmus	amāvimus	amātus
debēre	debēmus	debŭimus	debĭtus
molĕre	molĭmus	molŭimus	molĭtus
audīre	audīmus	audīvimus	audītus

words with proparoxytonic stress in Hispano-Romance contributed to the remaking of the IIIrd conjugation infinitive as well as other forms. These, then, are the major factors which determined the inability of these two conjugations to retain their distinctiveness: (1) the unfortunate stem stress of the IIIrd conjugation, (2) the lack of a distinctive perfect for both conjugations, and (3) the lack of a characteristic participle with a long vowel and consequent stress of that vowel giving the appearance of a suffix -V̄-to as opposed to -to. Furthermore, the loss of productivity in both conjugations was another negative point. (The one productive suffix in Hispano-Romance, derived from the IIIrd conjugation, -ecer, served only to further confuse the two conjugations as -ecer encroached on the territory of the IInd conjugation deadjectivals and denominatives resulting in the eventual loss of the semantic distinction between verbs like FLOREŌ, FLORĒRE 'to flower' and FLORESCŌ, FLORESCĔRE 'to begin to flower'.)

In returning to the concepts mentioned initially, productivity and simplicity, the vitality of conjugations I and IV (and their corresponding participles) is readily apparent. Yet many participles from conjugations II and III which have not undergone regularization enter Hispano-Romance and thrive. An explanation for this is wanting. To begin, it is obvious that high frequency verbs have a greater chance of conserving the etymological participle due to the existence of static expressions which are inherited in addition to a mere statistical reinforcement. Participles in Hispano-Romance which belong to this category are given in Figure 5 with their Latin etymon. The forms designated by an asterisk show remaking: -suelto, visto and vuelto. For visto the explanation is apparent through a brief comparison with the other forms. The participles in -so are largely eliminated in Hispano-Romance through regularization, but the verb ver being of high frequency develops an analogical irregular participle to replace its original irregular participle in VĪSUM. The remaking of VOLŪTUM and -SOLŪTUM (and their compounds) reveals again the rapid obsolescence of that class of participles which at one point seemed to be productive, namely the participles in -udo.

Figure 5.

'opened'	abierto	APERTUM
'covered'	cubierto	CO-OPERTUM
'said'	dicho	DICTUM
'written'	escrito	SCRIPTUM
'done'	hecho	FACTUM
'printed'	impreso	IMPRESSUM
'died'	muerto	MORTUUM
'put'	puesto	POSITUM
'(re-)solved'	*(re-)suelto	-SOLŪTUM
'seen'	*visto	VĪSUM
'returned'	*vuelto	VOLŪTUM

Menéndez Pidal (1941:322-323) informs his readers that the participle in -ŪTUS came to be 'la forma propia de conjugación -ĕre', flourished in the thirteenth century and 'vino muy luego a ser desusado en español'. However, the rapid decline of these forms as participles and their relegation to adjectival status[5] causes one to doubt their hegemony either in the thirteenth century or at any other time. The lack of forms such as *soludo attests to this. Furthermore, Hanssen (1945:120) restricts the participle in -udo geographically to the Leonese and Aragonese dialect areas, although he recognizes the occasional appearance of the form in the works of Alfonso X where it could well be a case of dialect interference rather than a Castilian form.

In addition to those verbs having only an irregular (with suffix other than -V̄-TUS) etymological or quasi-etymological past participle, there exists a large number of verbs with two 'participles', one etymological and irregular, the other analogical and regular. The former is usually obsolete, archaic or poetic for modern Spanish. A census of these verbs reveals some 70 simple verbs (120 including their compounds). Of this number, a surprisingly large portion belong to the Ist conjugation. However, this seemingly disconcerting fact may be partially explained. The majority of these -ar verbs are deverbative, derived from the p.p.p. of Latin verbs especially of the IIIrd conjugation. Traditionally, these etymological participles have been referred to as truncated. Their origin must be the occasional poetic usage described by Lindsay (1963:540) of an adjective in place of a participle. He further states that this use was extended into the Romance languages (especially the Eastern branch); thus one finds Ital. trovo beside trovato. This must be the phenomenon referred to by Menédez Pidal (1941:322) when he states that 'También para los verbos -ar hay un participio sin sufijo, muy común en italiano y no desconocido en el español dialectal, si bien con uso preferentemente adjetivo:

en el habla vulgar se dice "está pago"'. However, rather than a truncated or suffixless participle it would appear that one has here the completion of an analogy based on those -ar verbs which were derived from the etymological p.p.p of morphologically complex Latin verbs. Frequently the irregular participle remained in the language but was relexicalized as an adjective. The analogy, then, is formulated in this manner: junto:juntado::x:pagado, therefore x = pago.

Of the seventy verbs which comprise the list of verbs with two 'participles', many are intransitive. This, of course, eliminates the possibility of using the participle to create verb phrases in the passive voice, one of the major functions of the p.p.p. in Cl. Latin. Was this, however, its original and dominant function? Meillet and Vendryes (1948:360-361) propose that the original function of the p.p.p. was to supply a perfect for the medio-passives as well as the deponents (neither the IE aorist nor the perfect passed into Latin). From there, the participle was extended to the statives. The acquisition of a passive meaning, then, is a later development which eventually comes to affect even the deponents where forms like MERCĀTUS acquire the meaning 'having been bought' as well as the active meaning the deponent usually had in MERCĀTUS EST 'he has bought'. (It should be noted that the periphrastic passive in Latin was limited to the perfect system; but Hispano-Romance, having rejected the synthetic forms of the present system, generalized this construction throughout the paradigm, thus AMĀTUS EST 'he has been loved' > es amado 'he is loved'.)

The secondary function of the participle (adjectival) had already produced lexicalization of some participles in Cl. Latin (especially when the verb was infrequent or deficient), e.g. CITUS 'quick' and RATUS 'fixed'. This process was extended in Romance because of the desirability of separating the irregular participle from the verb paradigm after the creation of new regular forms. This delineation of functions corresponds exactly to Formule IV established by Kuryłowicz in 'Nature des procès dits "analogiques"' (1966:169):

> Quand à la suite d'une transformation morphologique une forme subit la différenciation, la forme nouvelle correspond à sa fonction primaire (de fondation), la forme ancienne est reservée pour la fonction secondaire (fondée).

If this is, indeed, the appropriate explanation for the lexicalization as adjectives of certain irregular participles, then the dichotomy derecho - dirigido, correcto (learned), correcho (archaic) - corregido is clearly understood. The short list given above of irregular participles in Hispano-Romance which were derived etymologically reflects those forms which survive as the unique participle of a verb on the strength of their frequency.

It remains to discuss the one new role of the participle in Hispano-Romance; that is, the formation of the perfect tenses with the auxiliary haber which is able to complement the participle by supplying the person and number attributes of the finite verb. The formation with haber + participle presents two problems: (1) concordance with a direct object either stated or implied, and (2) alternation with ser as auxiliary in the case of intransitive verbs. The first problem seems to be a reflex of the confusion of haber and tener. When haber was assigned the semantic and syntactic properties of tener, the following participle was reinterpreted as an adjective which modified and agreed with the direct object; for haber had now acquired the meaning of the transitive tener 'to hold, possess'. Confusion with the auxiliary ser in forming the perfect tenses is a rather vexing question, for it involves also the formation of the passive voice in Hispano-Romance.

The use of ser as an auxiliary in the formation of the perfect indicates a continuation of the primary function of the p.p.p. in Latin--to provide a perfect to the deponents and mediopassives. Although neither class of verbs survives as such in Hispano-Romance,[6] the use of ser in the perfect was clearly limited to intransitives. It appears that at some point these verb phrases with ser acquired a stative connotation, a recapitulation of the transition in Latin from perfect (mediopassive, deponent) to perfect passive of the construction p.p.p. + ESSE. The final result of this process in Hispano-Romance is a perfect with ser (present system only) + participle which shows agreement with the subject, alongside a passive (formed with SER + participle) inherited from Latin but lacking the perfective meaning of AMATUS EST 'he has been loved'. The loss of the synthetic forms of the Latin passive voice in the present system brought about the inconvenient syncretism in Hispano-Romance of the perfect of intransitive verbs and the passive voice of transitive verbs in the present tenses. Perhaps in an effort to distinguish the two grammatical aspects (active vs. passive and perfective vs. imperfective), the use of ser as an auxiliary began to diminish as haber was generalized throughout the system with the result that the perfect tenses were now characterized by haber + participle (nonagreement) and the passive voice by ser + participle (agreement).

Returning to the concept of primary and secondary functions, it is readily apparent from the previous discussion that the primary function of the participle in Hispano-Romance was a continuation of the Latin primary function, the formation of the perfect tenses. Since these formed part of the verb paradigm, the demand for regularity and conformity constituted a highly cogent force. As irregular participles were excluded from the paradigm, many were relegated to their secondary function as adjectives. This development was further facilitated by constructions in which irregular participles appeared in sentences with ser where that verb displayed its primary function--to serve as a copula which provided equivalence between subject and predicate (which frequently took the form of an adjective). As has been mentioned, such paraphrases had a stative connotation as did the parallel constructions with estar + participle. Under these circumstances, the irregular participle (lacking morphemic identity with the dominant class of participles in -V̄-TUS) was deprived of voice and tense, both necessary attributes of the true participle, as it lost its ties to the verb system and grew to be identified syntactically and semantically with the adjective. Thus the vitality of the new regularized participles in conjunction with the innovations in the verb system of Hispano-Romance combined to restrict the irregular etymological participle to its secondary function as an adjective.

NOTES

1. Some suffixes which formed Ist conjugation deverbative verbs in Latin were the diminutives -ILLĀRE, -LĀRE, and -CĀRE, as cited by Lindsay (1963:486-489) with these examples: SORBĒRE 'to swallow': SORBILLĀRE 'to sip', ŪRĒRE 'to scorch': USTULĀRE (p.p.p. ŪSTUS) 'to burn', FODĒRE 'to stab, goad': FODICĀRE 'to nudge'. Another suffix -ISSĀRE, -IDIĀRE, -IZĀRE, of Greek origin, offers several phonemic shapes depending upon chronology and lexical stratification (learned vs. popular). The Greek suffix was used originally to create denominatives and first entered Latin as -ISSĀRE, a form very dear to Plautus according to Väänänen (1971:96) who gives the verbs: GRAECISSĀRE 'to imitate the Greeks', MOECHISSĀRE 'to commit adultery', and PURPURISSĀRE 'to apply rouge'. Later Latin reintroduced the suffix in the forms -IZĀRE (learned) and -IDIĀRE (popular). The learned form is particularly prevalent in ecclesiastical language, e.g. BAPTIZARE, although forms such as BAPTIDIARE are also documented. Extension of the function of -IDIĀRE was to be expected as it provided a convenient vehicle for the formation of verbs, deadjectival and deverbative as well as denominal.

2. In Mignot's study, Les verbes denominatifs latins (1969:82-84), a list is provided of deadjectival verbs acquired in Latin between 100 B.C. and 600 A.D. The total of -ĒRE verbs given is surprisingly small: twenty-three verbs. They are largely derived from adjectives of the type CLARUS, A, UM 'clear' as in CLARĒRE 'to be clear', although there are occasionally verbs derived from third declension adjectives

such as PUTER, PUTRIS, PUTRIS 'rotten' in PUTRĒRE 'to reek'.

3. Some devices which distinguished the present stem were reduplication as in SISTŌ (cf. STŌ) 'I settle', nasal infix VINCŌ 'I conquer' and nasal suffix in CERNŌ 'I distinguish'. The perfect tenses and the p.p.p. showed the original stem: CRĒVĪ, CRĒTUS; VĪCĪ, VICTUS; STITĪ, STATUS. When these verbs passed into Hispano-Romance, the present stem was generalized necessitating the creation of new forms for the perfect and the past participle; thus Hispano-Romance has venzo, vencer, vencí, and vencido.

4. According to Lindsay (1963:334-336) the suffix *-to was used in the formation of (1) verbal adjectives which came to serve as the p.p.p., (2) ordinal numbers, e.g. SEX: SEX-TUS 'sixth', (3) abstract nouns in -T-ĀS such as CIVI-TĀ-S 'citizenry', (4) nouns indicating the product or result of an action where -to was added to -MEN as in VESTIMENTUM 'garment', and (5) verbal adjectives formed from nouns having the meaning 'provided with' as BARBĀTUS from BARBA 'beard'. Although adjectival in its origin, the p.p.p. differed from verbal adjectives of the type BARBĀTUS because as Brugmann (1902:319) notes, it had the properties of voice and tense, essential attributes of the verb. In addition, the p.p.p. was deverbative in its origin as opposed to the denominal BARBĀTUS.

5. In Old Spanish, participles in -udo are particularly abundant in verbs of mental action which normally lacked a direct object. Blaylock (1972:76-79) cites examples such as sabudo (infrequent next to sabido), entendudo, and conoçudo. He suggests that the vitality of such forms may be due to their use in set phrases such as conoçuda cosa sea, the standard incipit to legal texts of the 13th century. It is further suggested in Blaylock's study that this practice was the result of a Provençal influence, for Provençal as did most of the other Romance languages, retained a p.p.p in -ŪTUS which corresponded to IInd and IIIrd conjugation verbs with a perfect in -ŪĪ.

It should be noted that by Alfonsine times a fluctuation between the participle in -udo and the regularized -ido was apparent. Perhaps a further weakening of the -udo participles was a result of their identification with adjectives derived from fourth declension nouns which had a vocalism in -Ū-. The suffix was then reinterpreted to include the final vowel of the stem. The resultant suffix -ŪTUS began to drift semantically from the -TUS of forms like BARBĀTUS, and rather than meaning 'provided with', -ŪTUS indicated an excess or exaggeration of the quality connoted by the noun from which it was derived. Etymological cornudo (CORNŪTUM) differed little syntactically from the p.p.p. used as adjective. Thus the hypothetical case of un ome cornudo literally 'a horned man', figuratively 'a cuckold' next to un ome menudo 'a small man' (from etymological p.p.p. MINŪTUM) and un ome entendudo 'a learned man' (from unetymological *INTENDUTUM) demonstrates three parallel constructions in which both menudo and entendudo are entirely divorced from the verb paradigm, the first because there is no corresponding verb and the second because its environment seems to be in 'complementary distribution' with that of the rival form entendido (although there are cases of overlapping) which is generalized eventually in the participial (verbal) and adjectival functions.

6. It has been suggested by Professor **Henry Kahane** of the University of Illinois, who heard a version of this study presented at the Interdisciplinary Conference on 'Approaches to the Lexicon' (University of Louisville, March 10-11, 1977) that the reflexive verbs in Romance constitute to some degree a parallel to the **mediopassive**. Certainly the use of être as an auxiliary in the 'passé composé' of reflexive verbs in French is indicative of a differentiation of these verbs from the transitive verbs which employ avoir as an auxiliary. Furthermore, the syntactic behavior of the reflexives sets them apart from the intransitives (which also employ être in forming the 'passé composé') because they can take an object. The reflexive pronoun itself is normally a type of dative of interest rather than the direct object.

APPENDIX 1

See Figure 6, p. 120.

APPENDIX 2

To follow is an ordered list of data taken from literature of the court of Alfonso X (Solalinde 1922). These uses of the participle (regular, regularized, and irregular etymological) are shown:
  (1) Formation of the perfect with ser showing agreement with subject
  (2) Formation of the passive with ser showing agreement with subject
  (3) Formation of the perfect with haber showing agreement with direct object
  (4) Formation of perfect with haber showing no agreement
  (5) Adjectival function of the participle showing agreement with noun modified

Figure 6.

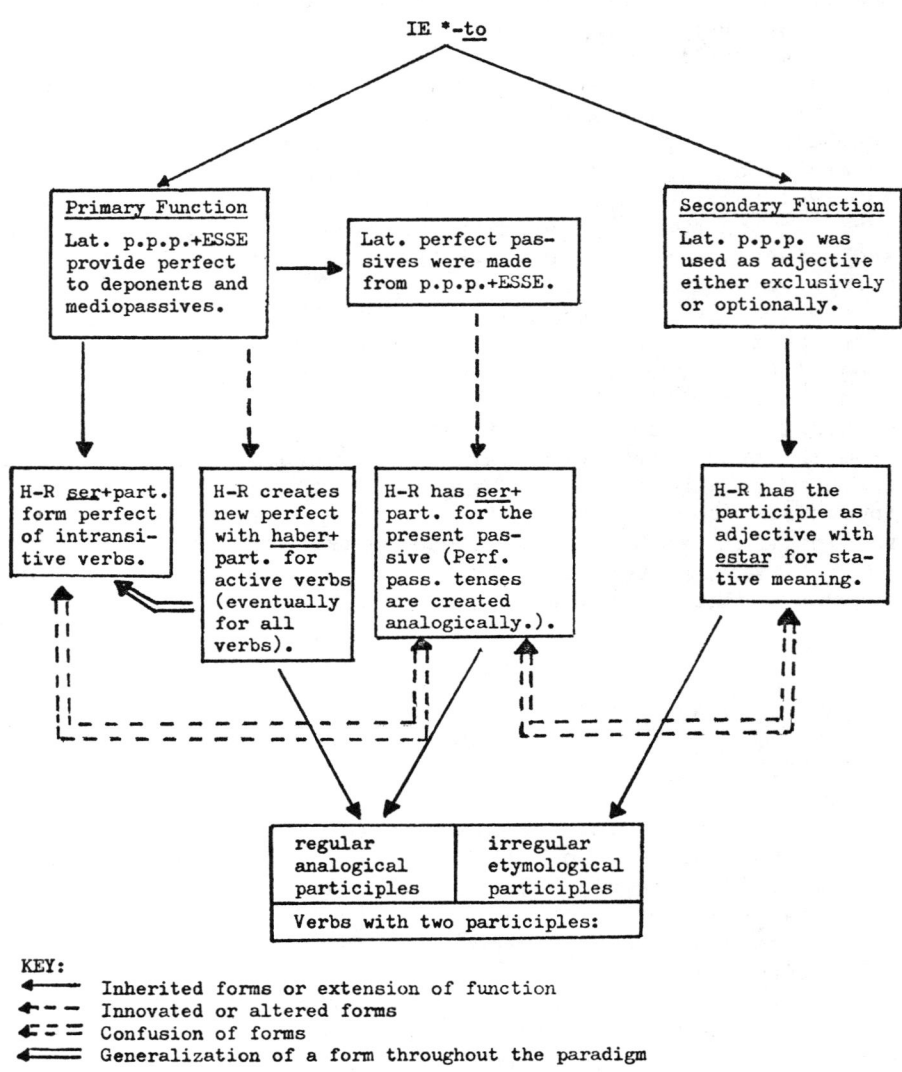

THE IRREGULAR PAST PARTICIPLE / 121

[vol.: page, line(s)]
(1) Perfect formation with <u>ser</u> (subject agreement).

   I: 141, 14-15   e por end cuando yo fuer <u>muerta</u>, tomaras el mio cuerpo e facell has ceniza
   I: 136, 29-30   ¿que mereció ell hermano de Yulo que aun no es <u>nacido</u>? (remaking of etymological NATUS)
   I: 61, 1-4   Quen leixal-a Groriosa/por moller que seia <u>nada</u>, macar seia mui fremosa/et rica et avondada (Galaico-Portuguese text, <u>nada</u> may be for the rhyme)

(2) Passive formation with <u>ser</u> (subject agreement).

   I: 184, 18-20   Adaulfo, rey de los godos, fue <u>muerto</u> a traición en Barcilona, et matol un su vasallo (<u>morir</u> here is transitive)
   I: 143, 7-9   e este fue a cinco mil et ciento et cincuaenta et dos anos que mundo et Adam fueron <u>fechos</u>
   I: 147, 15-17   Muchas veces avinie que, seyendo <u>vencida</u> la su haz, el solo la facie cobrar ca se paraba ante aquellos que fuien (remaking of VICTUS)

(3) Perfect formation with <u>haber</u> (direct object agreement).

   I: 143, 1-4   Despues que Julio Cesar hobo <u>muerto</u> a Pompeyo et <u>vencidos</u> sus enemigos et <u>conquistas</u> las gentes et las tierras, et <u>fechas</u> todas estas cosas que habedes <u>oidas</u> desuso
   I: 142, 17-18   E despues que las [palabras] hobo <u>dichas</u> muchas vegadas, tomo ell espada quel diera Eneas

(4) Perfect formation with <u>haber</u> (no agreement).

   I: 124, 11-13   Y Eneas, maguer que muchas veces viniera a aquel templo e viera las otras estorias no habie <u>visto</u> la de Troya.
   II: 173, 17-19   que nos de aqui adelante revocamos et desfacemos todos los otros testamentos que antes deste hobimos <u>fecho</u>.
   II: 22, 1-3   Et debenles facer lavar las manos ante de comer, porque sean limpios de las cosas que ante habien <u>tañido</u> (remaking of etymological TANGO, TACTUS)

*Haber extended as auxiliary to intransitive verbs (infrequent).

I: 135, 6-7   ¡Ay mezquina! ¡cuanto mal m'ha venido en este mundo!

I: 137, 1-4   Eneas, el poder que ha aquel dios que te face ir daquende, quisiera yo que hobiese otrosi quet ficiese que numcua aca hobiese venido

(5) Adjectival function (agreement with noun--These are all etymological forms which do not survive as participles).

I: 222, 14-15   Tollió el Senor todos los mayores de medio de mi, llamó el contra mi el tiempo por que crebante los míos escollechos. (EX+COLLECTUS)

I: 261, 9-10   E dexó alli a Abra su manceba libre et quita. (QUIETUS)

II: 78, 23-26   La primera que tiene la cabeza descubierta; la segunda que tiene los brazos descubiertos et las palmas tendudas; la tercera que esta vestida et cinta (tendudas, remaking of TENTUM; cinta from CINCTUS)

REFERENCES

Blaylock, Curtis. 1972. The -udo participles in Old Spanish. In: Homenaje a Antonio Tovar. Madrid: Gredos. 75-79.

Brugmann, Karl. 1902. Kurze vergleichende Grammatik. Berlin: Walter de Gruyter and Co.

Elcock, W. D. 1960. The Romance languages. London: Faber and Faber.

Ernout, Alfred. 1973. Elimination des formes anomales. In: Probleme der lateinische Grammatik. Edited by Klaus Strunk. Darmstadt: Wissenschaftliche Buchgesellschaft. 213-240.

Ernout, Alfred. 1920. Historische Formenlehre des Lateinischen. Translated by Hans Meltzer. Heidelberg: Carl Winters Universitätsbuchhandlung.

Hanssen, Federico. 1945. Gramática histórica de la lengua castellana. Buenos Aires: El Ateneo.

Kuryłowicz, Jerzy. 1964. The inflectional categories of Indo-European. Heidelberg: Carl Winters Universitätsverlag.

Kuryłowicz, Jerzy. 1966. Natures des procès dits 'analogiques'. In: Readings in linguistics II. Edited by Eric P. Hamp et al. Chicago: University of Chicago Press. 158-174.

Lausberg, Heinrich. 1966. Lingüística románica II. Morfología. Translated by J. Pérez Riesco and E. Pascual Rodríguez. Madrid: Gredos.
Lindsay, W. M. rprt. 1963 (1894). The Latin language. New York: Hafner Publishing Co.
Meillet, A. and J. Vendryes. 1948. Traité de grammaire comparée des langues classiques. Paris: Honoré Champion.
Menéndez Pidal, Ramón. 1941. Manual de gramática histórica española. 6th ed. Madrid: Espasa-Calpe, S.A.
Mignot, Xavier. 1969. Les verbes dénominatifs latins. Paris: Klincksieck.
Solalinde, Antonio G., ed. 1922. Alfonso X el Sabio: Antología de sus obras. 2 vols. Madrid: Colección Granada.
Väänänen, Veikko. 1971. Introducción al latín vulgar. Translated by Manuel Carrión. Madrid: Gredos.